Celebrate Piano!™

TEACHER'S GUIDE

Cathy Albergo

J. Mitzi Kolar

Mark Mrozinski

ISBN 0-88797-853-3

FREDERICK
HARRIS
MUSIC

Table of Contents

Oganization and Philosophy

I. OVERVIEW

Celebrate Piano!™ places the student at the center of the music learning experience. With each page, the authors guide the student to discover the joy of music. *Celebrate Piano!*™ provides a foundation of skills and understanding that allows for a lifelong participation in music.

Celebrate Piano!™ is a comprehensive piano method in four levels:

Lesson and Musicianship—1A, 1B, 2A, 2B, 3, 4
Solos—1, 2, 3 & 4
MIDI Disks and CDs—1A, 1B, 2A, 2B, 3, 4
Flashcards—1, 2, 3 & 4
Teacher's Guide

The four levels of books and materials encompass the crucial first years of study. Each *Lesson and Musicianship* book incorporates Repertoire, Finger Gyms (technique), Musicianship (reading and theory), Rhythm, Ear Skills, and Creativity. A separate *Solos* album for each level includes pieces that reinforce the elements and concepts presented in the *Lesson and Musicianship* book. These special recital or reward pieces will appeal to students, parents, and a recital audience.

This unique and innovative piano method is based on the latest pedagogical research, philosophy, and learning theory. *Celebrate Piano!*™ is a comprehensive method that prepares the student for a wide variety of musical styles including folk, jazz, and popular, and classical literature such as that found in *Celebration Series®, The Piano Odyssey®*.

Written primarily for the average-age beginner (6 or 7 years of age), *Celebrate Piano!*™ may also be used effectively with younger or older students. The method has been successfully tested in numerous teaching environments, including independent studios with individual and/or group lessons, university lab schools, and community music schools.

The following overview, "Elementary Piano Study—A Plan for Learning," shows the concepts and elements contained in each of the four levels. The general goals are to:
- establish musical literacy and rhythmic security
- develop the ability to hear what you see and see what you hear
- build a solid technical foundation
- cultivate creativity
- develop the ability to perform confidently
- establish good practice skills
- encourage independent learning
- foster a love of music of all styles

	LEVEL 1	LEVEL 2	LEVEL 3	LEVEL 4
Musicianship /Reading	• Non-staff reading • Low/middle/high • Up/down/same • Key and note names • Steps and skips • Harmonic and melodic 2nd, 3rd, 4th, 5th • Transposition • Grand staff, Treble and Bass clefs • Landmarks: Treble C, Middle C, Bass C, Treble G, Bass F • Line and space notes • Ledger lines • Dynamics: *p* and *f* • Phrase • Repeat sign • Measure, bar line, double bar line • Identification of repeated patterns • Sharp, flat, natural	• Landmarks: High C, Low C • Half and whole steps • Major 5-finger patterns • Tonic and Dominant • 8va • Dynamics: *pp, ff, mp, mf* • Crescendo, diminuendo • Accent • Intervals: 6th, 7th, octave • 5th–6th–5th accompaniment • Form: AB, ABA • D.C. al Fine • Introduction, coda • Key signatures: Major • Transposition	• 1st and 2nd ending • Sequence • IV chord • Harmonize with: I and V^7; i and V^7; I, IV, and V^7 • Perfect 4th, 5th, and octave • Minor 5-finger patterns and triads • Minor key signatures • Intervals: M3, m3; M2, m2; M6, m6 • Parallel and relative keys	• Intervals: M7, m7 • Chord inversions • Accompaniment styles in $\frac{3}{4}$, $\frac{4}{4}$, $\frac{6}{8}$ • Tenuto • Whole-tone scale • Pentatonic scale • Chromatic scale • Canon • Binary form • Major scales in tetrachords • Dominant 7th chord • iv chord • Harmonize with i, iv, and V^7 • Natural and harmonic minor scales
Rhythm	• Steady beat • Quarter, half, dotted half, whole notes • Quarter, half, whole rests • Tie • Time signatures: $\frac{2}{4}$, $\frac{3}{4}$, $\frac{4}{4}$	• Eighth note, dotted quarter-eighth, eighth rest • Upbeat: quarter and eighth note • Fermata • Ritardando, a tempo • Common time	• Time signatures: $\frac{6}{8}$, $\frac{9}{8}$ • Dotted quarter rest • Triplet	• Syncopation • Sixteenth notes and rests • Sixteenth-note combinations • Dotted eighth–sixteenth • Accelerando • Cut time, Alla breve
Technique	• LH and RH • Hand position • Finger numbers • Braced finger • Cluster • HT • Legato, staccato • Relaxed arm and wrist • 1–5 blocked • Contrary motion	• Major 5-finger patterns • Blocked (solid) and broken 5ths and 6ths • Crescendo, diminuendo • Finger crossing • Staccato vs. legato	• Two- and three-note slurs • Damper pedal • I, V^7 chords • Parallel motion with non-coordinated fingers • Minor 5-finger patterns and triads • Minor i, V^7 • Legato pedal • I–IV–I–V^7–I chord progression	• Chord inversion fingering • Major scales in tetrachords • Scale fingering rule • Scales—HS two octaves: C, G, D, A, E, and F Major • A minor (relative, natural, and harmonic) • Chromatic scale
Ear Skills	• Steady beat • Low/middle/high • Up/down/same • *p* and *f* • Quarter, half, dotted half, whole notes • Quarter, half, whole rests • Pattern identification • Harmonic and melodic 2nd, 3rd, 4th, 5th • Interval Safari • Clapbacks, playbacks • Legato and staccato • Relative pitch (Middle C) • Pitch dictation • Rhythmic dictation	• Interval Safari • Intervals: 6th, 7th • Octave • Add missing notes to melodies • Pitch notation within a 5-finger pattern • Solfège • Clapbacks, playbacks • Melodic dictation • Rhythmic dictation	• Interval Safari • Solfège • Melodic dictation • I and V^7 chords • Chord progression identification • Intervals: M3, m3; M2, m2; M6, m6 • Major vs. minor • Minor i and V^7 chords	• Interval Safari • Solfège • Melodic dictation • Harmonic dictation • Chord progression identification • Intervals: M7, m7 • Major vs. minor
Creativity	• Students compose their own pieces using concepts from Level 1 • Question and Answer • Improvisation	• Composition using concepts from Level 2 • Question and Answer: parallel and contrasting • Improvisation • Variation	• Question and Answer: Major and minor • Composition: ABA form • Improvisation • Variation	• Question and Answer: Major and minor • Composition: ABA form • Improvisation • Variation • Composition: Whole tone

PHILOSOPHY

Celebrate Piano!™ is a unit-based method with **performing, listening, describing, writing,** and **creating** consistently integrated into every unit. This integrated approach leads to the comprehensive musicianship that is vital to *Celebrate Piano!*™ and to the development of every young musician:

- The student **performs** by playing four to six compositions in each unit with musicality and technical proficiency.
- **Listening** includes perceiving, responding critically, and identifying elements heard.
- In **describing**, the student develops thinking skills and perception through discussion, practice, and self-evaluation.
- **Writing** activities provide opportunities for students to identify elements of music and demonstrate comprehension.
- By **creating**, the student applies imagination and understanding of musical elements and style to original improvisations or compositions.

The activities in these areas accommodate a variety of learning styles and provide a broad range of musical experiences, ensuring that every student will find their area of interest and achieve success. At the same time, the teacher is given ample opportunity to assess the student's comprehension and progress.

In addition to comprehensive musicianship, a primary component of *Celebrate Piano!*™ is conceptual learning. Concepts are the basic ideas or underlying principles of music. In learning basic concepts that grow progressively more sophisticated—identified as spiral learning—a student's musical understanding constantly evolves and becomes more complex. This natural sequence or hierarchy of concepts is integrative and interactive. The transfer of concepts from composition to composition enhances future learning, increases comprehension, provides continuity, improves memory, and leads to mastery of the subject. *Celebrate Piano!*™ also addresses the sequential development of technical skills, spatial and sensory understanding of the piano, and music notation.

Celebrate Piano!™ builds on the philosophies of Johann Friedrich Herbart, John Dewey, Jerome S. Bruner, Howard Gardner and others. The authors believe in fostering discovery learning through a carefully sequenced, spiral curriculum. Herbart's steps in learning have been adapted and simplified by many educators and are best known to piano teachers as **Preparation, Presentation,** and **Follow-up** (Reinforcement). These important steps have been carefully planned and written into *Celebrate Piano!*™ to provide an experience-before-symbol approach to learning. These steps may be further defined as follows:

Preparation—These activities allow students to hear and physically feel a musical element or concept one to four units before they see the symbol and before the element or concept is formally introduced and used in the repertoire. Elements that are being prepared are identified with a **preparation icon ▲.** Simply allow the student to experience the element without a detailed explanation, an introduction of the symbol, or terminology. Preparation often occurs in Ear-Skills activities, Finger Gyms, Musicianship or Creative activities.

Presentation—The teacher guides the student in discovering a new element or concept, names the element, and shows the symbol. When presented, a concept or element appears in a highlighted box at the top of the page. This new element is then included in the repertoire and activities.

Follow-up—Elements or concepts are reinforced through transfer, evaluation, and creative activities. Students demonstrate their understanding of new concepts and elements by using them in an improvisation, composition, or other areas of comprehensive musicianship.

READING APPROACH

The authors of *Celebrate Piano!*™ have created a unique combination of the intervallic/landmark and multiple-key approaches to help the student achieve a secure foundation in reading.

The student begins reading with a carefully sequenced introduction of intervals—2nds, 3rds, 5ths, and 4ths—independent of specific clefs. This assures a thorough grounding in intervallic reading, based on pattern recognition, prior to the introduction of the Treble and Bass clefs in Unit 8 of Level 1. Following the introduction of clefs, students are introduced to landmarks in the following order: Treble C, Middle C, Bass C, Treble G, Bass F, High C, and Low C. This order of presentation assures that the student will continue to develop as a strong reader.

The student regularly transposes to various hand positions that employ black and white keys. Through the use of keyboard charts in Level 1, the student plays in multiple Major keys, minor keys, and selected modes. In Level 2, the student continues to read and transpose 2nds, 3rds, 4ths, and 5ths; is introduced to 6ths, 7ths, and octaves; and plays in all twelve Major 5-finger patterns. In Level 3, the student learns the twelve minor 5-finger patterns. In Level 4, the student learns Major and minor scales in several keys and experiences whole-tone, pentatonic, and chromatic scales that begin on different pitches. In Levels 3 and 4, the student continues to transpose selected repertoire, harmonizations, and Finger Gyms to Major and minor keys.

ORGANIZATION

Celebrate Piano!™ is not taught page-by-page, but rather by sequencing the activities within each unit. Teachers will quickly become familiar with the placement and order of pedagogical areas within each unit.

New elements and concepts are experienced in activities prior to being presented in the repertoire. Each unit usually begins with a Finger Gym and Ear Skills activity. The pieces are grouped together in the center of the unit and are followed by reinforcement activities. Icons are used to identify each of the five areas of comprehensive musicianship as follows:

Finger Gym
technical exercises that develop physical skills

Musicianship
activities that reinforce reading and theory

Rhythm
activities that develop a sense of steady beat and reinforce rhythmic concepts

Ear Skills
activities that develop aural awareness

Creativity
activities that reinforce new elements and concepts and encourage students to compose and improvise

This unit order does not imply that the teacher should complete Ear Skills or Creativity last. In order to achieve a comprehensive approach, the teacher will select from the entire unit at each lesson.

Students will progress through the method at different rates. Some students may be able to complete an entire unit in one week, while others may require two weeks or more per unit.

The inclusion of all areas of musicianship, as well as repertoire, within one book, eliminates the need to coordinate several books per level in order to achieve comprehensive teaching.

The Scope and Sequence chart for each level (see p. 8), provides a snapshot of all the concepts, elements, and skills presented in each level, unit by unit.

SPECIAL FEATURES of *Celebrate Piano!*™ include:

Practice Plan—A Practice Plan found at the top of the page encourages the student to develop a good practice routine.

The abbreviation **T I P PS** is gradually introduced as a reminder for the student. These directions should be followed before playing a piece at the lesson and during practice at home:

T = Tap and ta the rhythm with a steady beat.
I   = Say the interval direction and size.
P = Find the phrases and repeated patterns.
PS = Play and say intervals, ta's, note names, or
      words.

For some pieces, students write their own Practice Plan, which helps them think about the piece, identify problem areas, and incorporate good practice habits.

You Be the Judge!—This activity encourages students to listen and evaluate their playing:

> Did you hear:
> ➤ ƒ?
> ➤ legato phrases?
> ➤ a steady beat?

Transpose—This musicianship activity reinforces reading and the multiple-key approach. For example, in Level 1, students play in ten Major keys, three minor keys, and the Lydian mode.

Interval Safari—Interval Safari is an ear-skills activity presented as part of a long-range ear-training plan. Through the introduction of the Middle C pitch and **Interval Safari** songs, the student enjoys learning the aural skills that are an essential part of musical training.

Echo Game–Clapbacks!—Rhythm clapbacks are an ear-skills activity in which the student echoes patterns that the teacher claps or taps using various rhythms. Clapbacks are also used as a preparation tool for new rhythmic concepts that have not been formally introduced.

Echo Game–Playbacks!—These short melodic phrases are used to help train the ear. The student copies or echoes a phrase played by the teacher. Playbacks are part of the long-term plan for developing aural awareness and response.

PLANNING YOUR LESSON

Planning each lesson ensures that the long-term musical goals and development of each student are achieved effectively and efficiently.

There are many areas to consider when lesson planning, whether for individual or group instruction. These include:

➤ Sequence:
  – conceptual teaching
  – Preparation, Presentation, Follow-up
  – comprehensive musicianship

➤ Repertoire and activities:
  – introduction of new pieces and activities
  – review
  – variety and flow in the lesson
  – off-bench and on-bench activities

➤ Class logistics:
  – number of students
  – learning styles
  – length of lesson—timing

Conceptual Learning/Teaching

The teacher may organize the lesson plan to focus on one concept comprehensively through related Finger Gym, Musicianship, Rhythm, Ear Skills, and Creative activities and Repertoire, before moving to another concept.

The authors have carefully sequenced the concepts within *Celebrate Piano!*™ and applied a basic outline for the Preparation, Presentation, and Follow-up of each concept. However, the actual execution rests with the teacher. Plan carefully and move between activities and repertoire with careful thought regarding transfer of conceptual learning and purpose. To provide assistance in planning each lesson, the discussion for each unit includes the following charts:

• **Planning for Preparation, Presentation, and Follow-up**

• **Unit Overview**—the Overview Chart lists each piece and activity and identifies the element being prepared or presented as well as special activities. The division of the unit is given to help teachers organize their lesson plan into one or two lessons.

• **Integrated Musicianship and Possible Sequence**—the Integrated Musicianship and Possible Sequence Chart groups activities within the unit that share a common or related concept or element and integrates the comprehensive musicianship.

Level 1

SCOPE AND SEQUENCE

UNIT	MUSICIANSHIP/READING	RHYTHM	TECHNIQUE	EAR SKILLS	CREATIVITY
LEVEL A					
1	• Exploring the keyboard • 1, 2, and 3 black keys • Low/middle/high	• Steady beat	• LH and RH finger numbers • Braced finger • Two- and three-note clusters	• Steady beat • Low/middle/high	• Create patterns
2	• Up/down/same • Transposition	• Quarter and half note	• Independent fingers 2, 3, 4	• Up/down/same • Soft and loud • Quarter and half note • Interval Safari: Middle C • Clapbacks, playbacks	• Composition: musical stories
3	• *p* and *f* • Phrase • Music staff • Line and space notes • Interval: 2nd or step		• Independent fingers 1, 2, 3	• Rhythmic identification: quarter and half note • 2nds	• Composition: musical stories
4	• Measure and bar lines • Music alphabet • CDE group • 2nds: melodic and harmonic • Letter clefs • Stem direction • Repeated patterns		• Legato • Hands together (HT) • Phrase	• 2nds: melodic and harmonic	• Composition: musical stories
5	• FGAB group • Interval: 3rd or skip, melodic and harmonic • Repeat sign		• Independent fingers 1, 2, 3, 4	• 3rds • Pattern recognition: 2nds and 3rds	• Composition: musical stories

Level 1 Scope and Sequence   *Celebrate Piano!*™ Teacher's Guide

UNIT	MUSICIANSHIP/READING	RHYTHM	TECHNIQUE	EAR SKILLS	CREATIVITY
6	• Combining 2nds and 3rds	• Dotted half and whole notes	• Fingers 1–3, 2–4	• Pitch dictation • Pattern recognition	• Question and Answer
LEVEL 1B					
7		• Time signatures: $\frac{2}{4}, \frac{3}{4}, \frac{4}{4}, \frac{6}{8}$	• Staccato	• Rhythmic dictation • Pitch dictation	• Question and Answer • Composition
8	• Grand staff • Treble and Bass clefs • Landmarks: Treble C, Middle C, Bass C		• Independent fingers 1, 2, 3, 4, 5	• Pitch dictation • Rhythmic dictation	• Question and Answer • Composition
9	• Ledger lines; contrary motion	• Rests: quarter, half, whole	• Contrary motion	• Pitch dictation	• Variation
10	• Landmarks: Treble G, Bass F • Interval: 5th, melodic and harmonic			• Rhythmic dictation • 5ths	• Question and Answer
11	• Sharp, flat, natural	• Tie		• Pitch dictation	• Question and Answer • Composition
12	• Interval: 4th, melodic and harmonic	• Time signatures: $\frac{2}{4}, \frac{3}{4}, \frac{4}{4}$	• Fingers 1–4; 2–5	• 4ths • Pitch dictation • Rhythmic dictation	• Question and Answer

LEVEL 1—UNIT 1: PLANNING FOR PREPARATION, PRESENTATION, AND FOLLOW-UP

Preparation	**Presentation**	**Follow-up**
• *p* and *f*	• Steady beat	
• Up/down/same	• LH and RH finger numbers	
• Independent fingers 2, 3	• 2 and 3 black keys	
	• Clusters	
	• Low/middle/high	
	• Braced finger	
	• Composition	

UNIT 1: OVERVIEW

PAGE	ACTIVITY	PRESENTATION	PREPARATION ▲	SPECIAL ACTIVITY	DIV.*
	Repertoire				
6	*Raindrops*	Steady beat; 2-note cluster			1
7	*Call of the Drum*	Steady beat; 3-note cluster			1
15	*The Ants Go Marching*	Steady beat; braced finger 3			2
	Solos				
2	*Tick Tock*	Steady beat, braced finger 2			1
3	*Asian Wind Chimes*	Steady beat, black keys, Braced finger 2			2
	Finger Gyms				
10	*Cluster Bounce*	Clusters	Up/down	Create	2
12	*Black-key Finger Workout*	Black keys	Up/down/same; **Ind. fingers 2, 3		2
	Musicianship				
4	*LH and RH Finger Numbers*	LH and RH finger numbers			1
4	*Finger Wiggle Game*	LH and RH finger numbers			1
5	*Exploring the Keyboard*	2 and 3 black-key groups			1
8	*Exploring Sounds*	Low/middle/high			2
9	*Low, Middle, High Patterns*	Low/middle/high		Create	2
11	*Finger Number Frolic*	LH and RH finger numbers			1
11	*Jumble o' Hands*	LH and RH			1
	Rhythm				
3	*Discover the Steady Beat*	Steady beat			1
	Ear Skills				
12	*Low, Middle, High Game*	Low/middle/high			2
	Creativity				
8	*Create the Sounds*	Low and high; composition			2
13	*Animal March*	Low and high	*p* and *f*		2

*   Div. = Division

** Ind. = Independent

Integrated Musicianship and Possible Sequence Charts

This chart divides the pieces and activities by element or concept. Using this chart a teacher can organize the lesson plan to focus on one concept comprehensively before moving on to another. The unit may be taught in one week or as suggested below in a two-week sequence as suggested below.

LEVEL 1—UNIT 1: INTEGRATED MUSICIANSHIP AND POSSIBLE SEQUENCE

Div. 1		Div. 2	
3	Discover the Steady Beat	12	Black-key Finger Workout
4	Finger Wiggle Game	14	The Ants Go Marching
11	Finger Number Frolic	8	Exploring Sounds
5	Exploring the Keyboard	8	Create the Sounds
11	Jumble o' Hands	9	Low, Middle, High Patterns
6	Raindrops	12	Low, Middle, High Game
7	Call of the Drum	13	Animal March
2—Solos 1	Tick Tock	10	Cluster Bounce
		3—Solos 1	Asian Wind Chimes

TEACHER'S NOTES AND TIPS

Many concepts are presented in Unit 1 because, for most students, everything is new! Students are introduced to basic reading and rhythmic concepts and learn to identify LH and RH symbols and experience keyboard geography—two and three black-key groups.

Repertoire

The melody line for all repertoire in Unit 1 is found in the upper part of the teacher's accompaniment. Encourage your student to sing the pieces. Be sure to maintain a steady beat when playing with your student (avoid adding a *rit.*).

When teaching a new piece, engage your student in a lively discussion about the title and how they might interpret the music to reflect the title. For example, in *Raindrops* (p. 6), is this a gentle rain, or a thunderstorm? Are the drums in *Call of the Drum* (p. 7) nearby, or in the distance?

Solos

Teachers may choose to integrate solos into the lesson plan for each corresponding unit, or they may decide to teach them after the unit in the *Lesson and Musicianship* book has been completed.

Rhythm

It is important to emphasize the concept of steady beat and chanting "ta" from the first lesson. The student should feel the beat of a piece before playing to help eliminate unsteady rhythms and start-and-stop playing. Be sure to "count off" in rhythm, with a steady beat, before the student plays or taps. You might say something like, "Ta, ta, play and ta." Encourage your students to do this at home. Use the closed keyboard cover as a surface for tapping and playing a piece before playing on the keyboard.

Movement

Young students need to change activities and positions frequently. Off-the-bench activities with large body movements such as walking, marching, arm swinging, conducting, and tapping help the student understand the concept of steady beat. These larger movements require that the students feel the beat in their entire body.

Encourage the student to make large strokes while drawing the lines to the steady beat in *Discover the Steady Beat* on p. 3. By drawing the beats in the book, on a blank sheet of paper, or on a chalkboard, the student is preparing to learn how to conduct the beat. The teacher may wish to repeat this activity elsewhere.

On p. 3 of Unit 1, students are encouraged to march to the beat of various songs played on a CD or MIDI, or by the teacher on the piano. You might choose *Yankee Doodle, When the Saints Go Marching In, Marine's Hymn, New River Train, It's a Small World, This Old Man,* or the CD or MIDI accompaniment of *The Ants Go Marching* or a song from a later unit of *Celebrate Piano!*™.

Technique

Finger Numbers
The introduction of LH, RH, and finger numbers is fun when the teacher creates interesting games or activities to reinforce these elements. You might play *Simon Says* and ask the student to:
- Wave the hand that the teacher calls
- Place the correct hand on top of your head, on your shoulder, etc.
- Wiggle the finger the teacher calls
- Tap the correct hand or finger in your lap, or tap individual fingers together with eyes closed

Hand Shape
Emphasize a good hand shape from the beginning. Even when playing clusters, a healthy hand shape is important. The fingers are lined up together in a closed hand position with the thumb rounded and tucked next to the index finger. Many teachers help young students by placing a small ball in the cupped hand. Some ask the student to imagine a small bird nestled in the palm of the hand and remind the student to treat it gently.

A good hand position will include a relaxed hand with the fingers resting lightly on the keys. A tense hand may produce fingers that "fly off the keys."

Ear Skills
Ear training activities are included throughout the method. At this point, the student should listen for a steady beat and begin to distinguish low, middle, and high sounds on the keyboard. Several recordings for children include excellent songs for dancing or walking to the beat and identifying low, middle, and high sounds.

Creativity
Creative activities not only reinforce new elements, they also provide the student with an opportunity for free expression and the chance to experiment.

The authors encourage students to create freely—they may want to "write" or graph a piece in the space provided or they may simply draw a picture that represents their composition.

Level 1—Unit 2: Planning for Preparation, Presentation, and Follow-up

Preparation
- *p* and *f*
- Interval: 2nds
- Legato
- Independent fingers 2, 3, 4

Presentation
- Quarter and half notes
- Up/down/same
- Independent fingers 2, 3, 4
- Transposition
- Middle C Safari
- Clapbacks, playbacks

Follow-up
- Black-key groups
- Low/middle/high
- Steady beat
- RH and LH
- Clusters
- Braced finger

Unit 2: Overview

Page	Activity	Presentation	Preparation ▲	Special Activity	Div.
	Repertoire				
17	*Swinging Monkeys*	Quarter and half notes			1
20	*Going Up and Down*	Up, down; quarter and half notes			1
22	*Rocket Ships*	Up; quarter and half notes; Ind. LH fingers 3, 2		*YBTJ!	2
23	*Boogie Down*	Up and down; quarter and half notes		Transpose	2
26	*Hot Cross Buns*	Up/down/same Ind. fingers 2, 3, 4			2
	Solos				
4	*Frog Hop*	Quarter and half notes; Up/down/same			1
5	*Lost in the Forest*	Ind. fingers 2, 3, 4; Up/down/same			1
	Finger Gyms				
16	*Rhythm Warm-ups*	Quarter and half notes			1
21	*2-3-4 Walk-a-bout*		Ind. fingers 2, 3, 4; legato; 2nds		2
	Musicianship				
18	*Up, Down, Same Game*	Up/down/same			1
19	*Connect the Hands*				1
	Rhythm				
16	*Clapping Patterns*	Quarter and half notes		** F1	1
	Ear Skills				
19	*Middle C Safari*	Middle C Song			1
24	*Hide and Seek Patterns*				2
24	*Echo Game—Clapbacks!*				1
24	*Echo Game—Playbacks!*	Ind. fingers 2, 3, 4	2nds		1
	Creativity				
21	*Soft or Loud?*		*p* and *f*		2
25	*The Elephant and the Mouse*		*p* and *f*		2

*   YBTJ = You Be the Judge!
**   F1   = Flashcards set 1

LEVEL 1—UNIT 2: INTEGRATED MUSICIANSHIP AND POSSIBLE SEQUENCE

Div. 1			Div. 2		
19	*Connect the Hands*		21	*2–3–4 Walk-a-bout*	
24	*Echo Game—Clapbacks!*		24	*Hide and Seek Patterns*	
16	*Clapping Patterns*		21	*Soft or Loud*	
16	*Rhythm Warm-ups*		22	*Rocket Ships*	
17	*Swinging Monkeys*		23	*Boogie Down*	
24	*Echo Game—Playbacks!*		25	*The Elephant and the Mouse*	
18	*Up, Down, Same Game*		26	*Hot Cross Buns*	
20	*Going Up and Down*		5—Solos 1	*Lost in the Forest*	
4—Solos 1	*Frog Hop*				
19	*Middle C Safari*				

TEACHER'S NOTES AND TIPS

The primary elements in Unit 2 are the introduction of quarter and half notes; counting with ta and ta-ah; up, down, same; and the introduction of ear training.

Musicianship

Transpose
Transposition is a musicianship skill that reinforces reading and the multiple-key approach. The authors of *Celebrate Piano!*™ introduce transposition step by step and have carefully selected the pieces and Finger Gyms for transposition.
• The pieces in Level 1 are transposed by simply moving the hand from a black-key group to a white-key group and vice versa. Keyboard graphics (see p. 33) are sometimes used to illustrate a new hand position.
• After the introduction of 5-finger patterns in Unit 3 of Level 2A, the student is asked to move from one 5-finger pattern to another.
• After the introduction of sharp key signatures in Unit 6 of Level 2A, students are asked to move from one key to another. Transposition continues throughout Levels 3 and 4.

You Be the Judge!
This activity encourages and reminds students to always listen carefully and critically as they play. If students are able to hear and relate what and how they are actually playing to the written score, they are more able to recognize errors and make corrections.

Rhythm
Students are introduced to quarter notes, half notes, and syllabic counting in this unit. They should be

encouraged to say "ta" or "ta-ah" aloud as they play. Syllabic counting gives students a secure sense of pulse and duration. The verbal attack of the "T" in Ta, or the continuation of the beat in Ta-ah for a half note, is easy for students to feel and perform with accuracy. Syllabic counting also helps eliminate confusion between finger numbers and counting numbers.

When clapping half notes, the student should move on the second beat to illustrate the ongoing sound of a half note (e.g., move the clasped hands to the chest or pulse in the air on beat two).

Movement
Games make learning new concepts fun. Here are some ideas.

Create a marching or stepping game to match the rhythm of a piece. For example: *Swinging Monkeys* (p. 17).
• For each quarter note: step forward
• For each half note: bend the knees on beat one and straighten up on beat 2

Create a stretching game to match low, middle, and high sounds played by the teacher:
• High sounds—have the student stretch and reach to the sky with the hands
• Middle sounds—have the student place their hands on their waist
• Low sounds—have the student touch their toes or squat and touch the floor

Ear Skills

Ear training is crucial to the development of good sight-reading skills and general musicianship.

Interval Safari

Middle C Safari, and the introduction of the *Middle C Song* is the beginning of a long-range ear-training plan called *Interval Safari*. This is an activity or game for the student in which animal characters are identified with a particular interval. Each interval has its own special animal song.

We begin with the Middle C character, a friendly sheepdog who will be our guide as we discover new intervals.

Help your student locate and play Middle C the first time. Students are asked to play Middle C on the piano to reinforce the sound and location only. The primary focus is the voice, matching pitch, and developing a strong sense of relative pitch. Spend only a short time on this drill—only as long as it takes to sing the song and see if the student is singing on pitch—but repeat it several times throughout the lesson. Middle C has been chosen as the first pitch to sing to allow for a comfortable singing range up to an octave above Middle C.

Have your student play this special game at home: *every* time they walk past the piano ask them to pause, sing the *Middle C Song*, and play Middle C to see if they are singing in tune. (Remind parents of the importance of having a tuned piano at home.)

The goal is to sing Middle C on demand without hearing it first. Frequently students match the pitch within a couple of weeks; most become proficient at matching Middle C within the first six months of lessons. Consistently coming within a half step of Middle C should be considered a success. Constant weekly reinforcement of this activity at home and in the lesson is the key to success.

Echo Game—Clapbacks!
and *Echo Game—Playbacks!*
Clapbacks and playbacks are a valuable teaching tool. These activities can be completely spontaneous or can be carefully planned by the teacher. They should only take one or two minutes of lesson time.

The examples for the teacher in each unit of the *Lesson and Musicianship* book are merely suggestions. Teachers are encouraged to create their own clapbacks and playbacks and do as many as needed for reinforcement.

Clapbacks: The teacher claps a short rhythmic pattern. The student then immediately claps the same pattern back. Repeat, using a different pattern. In future lessons, you may ask the student to chant the ta's or to notate the pattern.

Playbacks: The teacher plays a pattern on 2 or 3 black keys. The student echoes the pattern by playing it on the piano. The student should not see the teacher's hands.

Creativity

In many of the creative activities, students are asked to "Draw your song in any way you like!" Students and teachers should take this literally—anything the student draws is acceptable. Many students simply want to draw pictures of their pieces or the subjects of their pieces. Some may want to try to notate their piece. They should be free to use the space provided creatively.

Tips:

Middle C Safari (p. 19)
Have the student give the sheepdog character a name that begins with the letter C. (The authors of *Celebrate Piano!*™ call this character Charlie.)

Rocket Ships (p. 22)
Enrichment activity: Circle the first seven notes and ask your student to find a similar pattern.

Boogie Down (p. 23)
The student must move back up the octave to prepare to play the second verse.

Hide and Seek Patterns (p. 24)
If you want to repeat this activity several times, have the student point to the correct answer rather than circling it.

LEVEL 1—UNIT 3: PLANNING FOR PREPARATION, PRESENTATION, AND FOLLOW-UP

Preparation
- 2nds
- Music alphabet
- Dotted half note
- Legato
- Hands together (HT)
- Independent fingers 1, 2, 3

Presentation
- Music staff
- Line notes and space notes
- Interval: 2nd or step
- Dynamics: *p* and *f*
- Phrase

Follow-up
- Up/down/same
- Low/middle/high
- Black-key groups
- Steady beat
- Quarter and half notes
- RH and LH
- Finger numbers
- Middle C

UNIT 3: OVERVIEW

PAGE	ACTIVITY	PRESENTATION	PREPARATION ▲	SPECIAL ACTIVITY	DIV.
	Repertoire				
31	*Deep Blue Sea*	2nds		Transpose	1
32	*Whisper or Shout*	*p*, *f*; 2nds		YBTJ!	1
33	*Brass Band*	*f*; 2nds		Transpose	2
34	*Clouds*	Phrase; *p*; 2nds		Transpose	2
39	*Prairie Song*	Phrase; *p*; 2nds		YBTJ!	2
	Solos				
6	*Carousel Waltz*	*f*; 2nds			1
7	*Lullaby*	Phrase; *p*; 2nds			2
	Finger Gyms				
27	*Left–Right–Both Workout!*		HT; 2nds		1
35	*Fun Thumb Phrases!!*	Phrase; *p*; 2nds	Legato; ind. fingers 1, 2, 3	Transpose	2
	Musicianship				
28	*Line Note or Space Note?*	Music staff; line and space notes			1
28	*Drawing Notes*	Line and space notes			1
29	*Discovering 2nds*	2nds		F2	1
30	*Stepping Along*	2nds			1
35	*2nd Chance*	2nds			2
35	*Alphabet Cheer!*		Music alphabet		2
	Rhythm				
36	*Rhythm Taps*			Create	1
	Ear Skills				
27	*Middle C Safari*				1
36	*Interval Safari: Busy Bee Song*	2nd			1
37	*Game o' Listening*				2
37	*Echo Game—Clapbacks!*		Dotted half note		2
37	*Echo Game—Playbacks!*	Phrase; *p*; 2nds	Dotted half note		1
	Creativity				
38	*My Day at the Circus*				2

LEVEL 1—UNIT 3: INTEGRATED MUSICIANSHIP AND POSSIBLE SEQUENCE

Div. 1		Div. 2	
27	*Left–Right–Both Workout!*	37	*Echo Game—Clapbacks!*
36	*Rhythm Taps*	37	*Game o' Listening*
28	*Line Note or Space Note?*	33	*Brass Band*
28	*Drawing Notes*	35	*2nd Chance*
29	*Discovering 2nds*	38	*My Day at the Circus*
30	*Stepping Along*	34	*Clouds*
31	*Deep Blue Sea*	35	*Fun Thumb Phrases!*
27	*Middle C Safari*	39	*Prairie Song*
36	*Interval Safari: Busy Bee Song*	7—Solos 1	*Lullaby*
37	*Echo Song—Playbacks*	35	*Alphabet Cheer!*
32	*Whisper or Shout*		
6—Solos 1	*Carousel Waltz*		

TEACHER'S NOTES AND TIPS

Reading

Intervallic and directional reading is introduced in Unit 3 with the presentation of the staff, line and space notes, and the interval of a 2nd. Students need to begin their reading experience by recognizing that notes move up or down and that they move a certain distance.

Saying the interval direction and size before they play, becomes a regular part of the Practice Plan. Students may play the piece in their lap, on the keyboard cover, or "in the air," as they chant ("start, up a 2nd, down a 2nd," etc.). These activities give students a physical sense of direction and highlight the fingers they will use before they play their piece on the piano.

By using the principles of intervallic and directional reading, students can read quickly and easily anywhere on the keyboard, and transpose with ease. Teachers and parents are cautioned to avoid naming the lines and spaces as this slows down the reading process and interferes with the student's ability to concentrate on the interval and direction. Note naming should be introduced and reinforced with flashcards after the presentation of the Grand staff and landmarks in Level 1B, Unit 8.

Movement

When singing or chanting interval direction and size, students can use large arm motions to draw the directional shape of pieces in the air.

Musicianship

Phrasing

Expressive playing and phrasing is an essential part of piano lessons. Although students may take some time before they master the art of shaping a phrase, they can understand that the last note in a phrase should be played softly and that they should breath or lift between phrases. Have your student listen as you model beautiful phrases.

Practice Plan

In order to encourage good practice habits, the authors begin introducing abbreviations for specific activities. In Unit 3, the student learns: **T** = Tap and ta the rhythm with a steady beat. These directions should be followed both at the lesson and at home.

Ear Skills

Interval: 2nd

The *Busy Bee Song* uses 2nds. Students are encouraged to sing this song several times a day, starting from Middle C. The goal is to instill the sound of a Major 2nd in the ear.

Tips:

Clouds (p. 34)

To reinforce the performance of the phrase, add the word "lift" when chanting. For example, chant "ta, lift" on the last half note in each phrase.

Drawing Notes (p. 28)

Specific instructions for drawing notes have not been given because stem direction is not a major concern at this point. However, the teacher may provide some guidance regarding stem placement and direction. The stem direction rule appears later.

LEVEL 1—UNIT 4: PLANNING FOR PREPARATION, PRESENTATION, AND FOLLOW-UP

Preparation
- FGAB group
- Legato
- Interval: 3rd or skip
- Dotted half and whole notes
- Independent fingers 1, 2, 3, 4
- Fingers 2–4

Presentation
- Two staffs
- Measure, bar line
- Legato
- Melodic and harmonic 2nds
- Repeated patterns
- Music alphabet
- Letter clefs
- CDE group
- HT
- Stem direction

Follow-up
- *p* and *f*
- Line and space notes
- Phrase
- Low/middle/high
- Up/down/same
- Quarter and half notes
- Steady beat
- Finger numbers 2, 3, 4
- Middle C

UNIT 4: OVERVIEW

PAGE	ACTIVITY	PRESENTATION	PREPARATION ▲	SPECIAL ACTIVITY	DIV.
	Repertoire				
42	Lullaby	Legato; two staffs		Transpose	1
45	Busy Bee Toccata	Mel.* and har.** 2nds; repeated patterns			1
47	Alphabet Song	Stem direction; music alphabet; letter clefs			1
49	CDE Waltz	CDE; repeated patterns; letter clefs		YBTJ!	2
50	Scooter	CDE; letter clefs		Transpose	2
55	Merrily We Roll Along	HT; CDE; letter clefs		Transpose	2
	Solos				
8	My Friend, Ling Soo	Legato; repeated patterns; mel. and har. 2nds			1
9	Alphabet Soup	Mel. and har. 2nds; CDE; letter clefs; music alphabet			2
	Finger Gyms				
40	Two-staff Stepping	Two staffs	Legato		1
48	Phrase the Legato	CDE	3rds; fingers 2–4		2
51	Hands Together Challenge	HT			2
	Musicianship				
41	Bar Line Search	Measure and bar lines		F3	1
43	Wait . . . A Second!	Mel. and har. 2nds		F4	1
44	Pattern Search	Repeated patterns			1
46	Naming the White Keys	Music alphabet			1
46	Alphabet Speller	Music alphabet			1
48	Alphabet Hunt	CDE group			2
51	Bar Line Discovery	Measure and bar lines			2
52	Follow the 2nd	2nds			1
	Rhythm				
52	Reading Rhythms			Create	1
	Ear Skills				
40	Interval Safari				1
53	What Do You Hear?	Mel. and har. 2nds			2
53	Echo Game—Clapbacks!		Dotted half and whole note		1
53	Echo Game—Playbacks!		FGAB; ind. fingers 1, 2, 3, 4		2
	Creativity				
54	Mountain Climbing				2

* mel. = melodic
** har. = harmonic

LEVEL 1—UNIT 4: INTEGRATED MUSICIANSHIP AND POSSIBLE SEQUENCE

Div. 1		Div. 2	
53	*Echo Game—Clapbacks!*	51	*Bar Line Discovery*
52	*Reading Rhythms*	48	*Alphabet Hunt*
52	*Follow the 2nd*	48	*Phrase the Legato*
40	*Two-staff Stepping*	49	*CDE Waltz*
40	*Interval Safari*	50	*Scooter*
41	*Bar Line Search*	54	*Mountain Climbing*
42	*Lullaby*	51	*Hands Together Challenge*
43	*Wait . . . A Second!*	55	*Merrily We Roll Along*
44	*Pattern Search*	9—Solos 1	*Alphabet Soup*
45	*Busy Bee Toccata*	53	*What Do You Hear?*
8—Solos 1	*My Friend, Ling Soo*	53	*Echo Game—Playbacks!*
46	*Naming the White Keys*		
46	*Alphabet Speller*		
47	*Alphabet Song*		

TEACHER'S NOTES AND TIPS

Many new elements are presented in Unit 4. Teachers may need to spend two or even three lessons on this unit.

Musicianship
Repeated patterns
Students need to begin recognizing repeated patterns as soon as possible. This skill helps foster good reading habits and prepares students to identify form.

Letter Clefs
Students learn the music alphabet in this unit. Letter clefs relate the alphabet to the staff and aid students in finding their beginning hand position. Letter clefs always identify the starting note.

Teachers should remember that one of the focuses of this method is intervallic reading. After finding the starting position from a keyboard icon or from a letter clef, the student can easily read the interval direction and distance. Students can transpose with ease because the intervals remain the same in a new key—only the hand position changes.

There is no need to add the names of lines and spaces or to add treble and bass clefs. This would confuse the reading approach and slow the development of true intervallic reading.

Clefs will be added in Level 1B when landmarks are presented. At this point, students begin to learn the landmark notes and name the notes and intervals surrounding them.

The Music Alphabet
On p. 46, students learn the music alphabet. They require numerous repetitions of the music alphabet in order to securely repeat the alphabet comfortably. Create keyboard drills that require the student to recite the alphabet rapidly forward and backward. This requires only seconds of lesson time.

Two Staffs
Until now, the student has been reading the RH and LH notes on one staff to facilitate eye movement from left to right. In Unit 4, each hand is given its own staff.

In *Two-staff Stepping* (p. 40), the teacher will need to assist the student in reading from left to right, with the eyes shifting to the lower staff after the RH plays. From this point forward, the student will be challenged to develop eye movement from staff to staff as an integral part of HT playing.

Technique
Legato
We encourage a continuous, patient development of this finer finger skill by walking from finger to finger. Try demonstrating legato finger movement on the student's forearm as well as on the piano. Legato can also be demonstrated using larger body motions:
• Have the student jump or hop from foot to foot
• To demonstrate legato, have the student walk lightly from foot to foot, with no excess movement
The musical performance of legato phrases is integral to the student's expressive growth.

Hands Together Playing
The development of HT playing has been carefully sequenced to provide for security in later levels and the progression to standard repertoire.

In Unit 3, p. 27, the student learned a Finger Gym that prepared them to play HT with coordinated fingers (fingers 2). Once students are familiar with reading on two staffs, they can begin playing HT. Initially, the student plays HT with coordinated fingers, such as the two finger 3's in *Hands Together Challenge*, Example 1 (p. 51). In the second example of this Finger Gym, the number of notes that use coordinated fingers is increased. In addition, the use of HT begins with the same rhythmic values in both hands. These Finger Gyms prepare students to play fingers 3 together in *Merrily We Roll Along* (p. 55).

Students play with coordinated fingers naturally. The pieces are designed to use the strong fingers of their young hands. Students continue to play with coordinated fingers in the units that follow. In *FGAB Polka* (Unit 5, p. 59), the student plays a LH cluster with fingers 2 and 3, which coordinates with RH finger 3. The first planned use of different fingers while playing HT occurs in *Whole-note Cheer* in Unit 6 (p. 72). A note is repeated in the LH while the RH uses a different finger. In preparation for hand independence, the student encounters HT playing with different fingers in Levels 2, 3, and 4.

Finger Gyms
You may notice that some Finger Gyms are still notated "off-staff" even though the staff was introduced in Unit 3. The student *experiences* a new concept before seeing it notated. For example, *Phrase the Legato* on p. 48 is notated off-staff because it prepares the interval of a 3rd.

LEVEL 1—UNIT 5: PLANNING FOR PREPARATION, PRESENTATION, AND FOLLOW-UP

Preparation
- 3rds
- Independent fingers 1, 2, 3, 4
- Staccato
- Combining 2nds and 3rds
- Dotted half notes and whole notes
- Fingers 1–3; 2–4

Presentation
- Independent fingers 1, 2, 3, 4
- FGAB group
- Interval 3rd or skip: melodic and harmonic
- Repeat sign
- Fingers 1–3; 2–4

Follow-up
- *p* and *f*
- 2nds: melodic and harmonic
- Staff, measure, bar line
- Repeated patterns
- Phrase
- Quarter and half notes
- Legato
- HT
- Middle C

UNIT 5: Overview

PAGE	ACTIVITY	PRESENTATION	PREPARATION ▲	SPECIAL ACTIVITY	DIV.
	Repertoire				
58	*Flying*	FGAB; fingers 1, 2, 3, 4		YBTJ!	1
59	*FGAB Polka*	FGAB; fingers 1, 2, 3, 4			1
61	*Trombones*	3rds; 1–3		YBTJ!	2
62	*Fuzzy Caterpillar*	Repeat sign; 3rds; 1–3		Transpose	2
67	*Cuckoo Bird Concert*	Mel. and har. 3rds; 2–4		Transpose	2
	Solos				
10	*Starlight, Star Bright*				1
11	*Cancan*	Mel. and har. 3rds; 1–3			2
	Finger Gyms				
56	*Finger Aerobics*		Ind. fingers 1, 2, 3, 4; 3rds; staccato; 1–3; 2–4		1
63	*Legato Warm-up*	Mel. and har. 3rds; repeat sign; 2–4		F5	2
	Musicianship				
57	*Alphabet Hunt*	FGAB			1
57	*FGAB Family Members*	FGAB			1
60	*Discovering 3rds*	3rd			2
64	*Word Search*				1
	Rhythm				
64	*Tapping Game*				1
	Ear Skills				
56	*Interval Safari*				1
63	*Interval Safari: Cuckoo Bird Song*	3rds			2
65	*Pattern Detective*				1
65	*Echo Game—Clapbacks!*		Dotted half and whole notes		1
65	*Echo Game—Playbacks!*		Combining 2nds and 3rds		2
	Creativity				
66	*Dancing Letters*				2

LEVEL 1—UNIT 5: INTEGRATED MUSICIANSHIP AND POSSIBLE SEQUENCE

Div. 1			Div. 2		
64	*Tapping Game*		65	*Echo Game—Playbacks!*	
65	*Echo Game—Clapbacks!*		60	*Discovering 3rds*	
64	*Word Search*		63	*Interval Safari: Cuckoo Bird Song*	
10—Solos 1	*Starlight, Star Bright*		61	*Trombones*	
56	*Finger Aerobics*		62	*Fuzzy Caterpillar*	
57	*Alphabet Hunt*		66	*Dancing Letters*	
57	*FGAB Family Members*		63	*Legato Warm-up*	
58	*Flying*		67	*Cuckoo Bird Concert*	
59	*FGAB Polka*		11—Solos 1	*Cancan*	
65	*Pattern Detective*				
56	*Interval Safari*				

TEACHER'S NOTES AND TIPS

Musicianship

Interval: 3rd

The introduction of melodic and harmonic 3rds continues the development of intervallic and directional reading. Students need to recognize that 3rds skip from a line to a line or a space to a space on the staff, skip a white key on the keyboard, and skip a finger in the hand (1–3; 2–4; 3–5). Students should continue to say the interval direction and size as they read.

Interval Game

Many clever games can be created to reinforce intervals, note names, and fingering. For example, you might try a *Simon Says* type of game in which students close their eyes and follow your directions.

Example 1—note names:
Start on G; Go up a 2nd, up a 2nd; up a 3rd; down a 2nd. Where are you? (C)
At the end, have the students call out the answer.

Example 2—finger numbers:
Start on LH finger 1; go down a 3rd; down a 3rd; up a 2nd. Which finger did you land on? (Finger 4) Students can hold their hands in the air so that you can see the correct response.

Encourage students to respond quickly and automatically to your directions, thereby reinforcing intervals, note names, and fingering. Students love to go faster and faster with this game!

Write your own Practice Plan

On p. 58, the student is asked to write a Practice Plan for *Flying*. This activity is intended to help students understand the importance of a good practice routine. The teacher may need to help with this activity at first. Review the Practice Plans for *CDE Waltz* or *Scooter* with your students for ideas.

Technique

Discuss how to use the thumb when teaching *Flying* (p. 58). The hand plays with a relaxed, rounded position, while the thumb plays parallel to the nail on its side. Encourage the student to draw or pull the thumb down rather than lifting and striking the key with the thumb.

Ear Skills

When focusing on ear training activities, be sure to play a combination of melodic and harmonic intervals for students to identify. Begin by playing the intervals from Middle C until the student is confident; then play intervals from other places on the keyboard. Remember, the student should not see the keyboard during these ear training exercises.

Students should continue to sing the Middle C pitch, interval songs, and finger numbers, note names, or the words to their songs. Linking the voice and body to musical notation and the ear helps the student to hear what they see and see what they hear.

LEVEL 1—UNIT 6: PLANNING FOR PREPARATION, PRESENTATION, AND FOLLOW-UP

Preparation
- Landmark C's
- Staccato

Presentation
- Combining 2nds and 3rds
- Dotted half note
- Whole note
- Pitch dictation
- Question and Answer

Follow-up
- 2nds; 3rds
- Music alphabet
- Letter clefs
- Repeat sign
- Legato
- HT
- 1, 2, 3, 4; 1–3; 2–4

UNIT 6: OVERVIEW

PAGE	ACTIVITY	PRESENTATION	PREPARATION ▲	SPECIAL ACTIVITY	DIV.
	Repertoire				
69	*Toy Soldier March*	2nds and 3rds		YBTJ!	1
71	*My New Bike*	Dotted half; 2nds and 3rds		Transpose	1
72	*Whole-note Cheer*	Whole note; 2nds and 3rds		YBTJ!	2
73	*Old MacDonald*	Dotted half, whole notes		Transpose; Create	2
78	*The Echo Song*	2nds and 3rds			2
	Solos				
12	*Rover*	2nds and 3rds			1
13	*Fairy Tale*	2nds and 3rds			2
	Finger Gyms				
68	*Finger Warm-ups*	2nds and 3rds		F6	1
74	*Interval Dance*	2nds and 3rds	Staccato		2
	Musicianship				
74	*Word Search*				1
74	*Tic-Tac-Toe*		Landmark C's		2
	Rhythm				
70	*Rockin' Rhythms*	Dotted half and whole notes		F7	1
70	*Tapping Rhythms*	Dotted half and whole notes		Create	2
75	*Rhythm Maze*	Dotted half and whole notes			2
	Ear Skills				
68	*Interval Safari*				1
76	*Listening Game*				1
76	*Echo Game—Clapbacks!*				1
76	*Echo Game—Playbacks!*	2nds and 3rds			2
77	*Pattern Detective*				2
	Creativity				
77	*Question and Answer*	Question and Answer; improvisation on CDE			1

LEVEL 1—UNIT 6: INTEGRATED MUSICIANSHIP AND POSSIBLE SEQUENCE

Div. 1			Div. 2		
68		*Interval Safari*	74		*Tic-Tac-Toe*
76		*Listening Game*	76		*Echo Game—Playbacks!*
68		*Finger Warm-ups*	77		*Pattern Detective*
69		*Toy Soldier March*	13—Solos 1		*Fairy Tale*
12—Solos 1		*Rover*	74		*Interval Dance*
77		*Question and Answer*	78		*The Echo Song*
76		*Echo Game—Clapbacks!*	70		*Tapping Rhythms*
70		*Rockin' Rhythms*	72		*Whole-note Cheer*
71		*My New Bike*	73		*Old MacDonald*
74		*Word Search*	75		*Rhythm Maze*

TEACHER'S NOTES AND TIPS

Important elements in Unit 6 are the addition of the dotted half note and whole note, and the combining of 2nds and 3rds in the repertoire.

Movement

The student should continue to shape melodies in the air, choosing different spatial distances to distinguish 2nds from 3rds. For example, *Finger Warm-ups* (p. 68):

- Place the right arm at waist level to represent the beginning note
- Move slightly higher for the 2nd up and slightly lower for the 2nd down
- Move up a larger distance for 3rds
- Use the left arm to shape the last two measures since the LH plays these measures

Ear Skills

Listening Game (p. 76) is the first example of pitch dictation. Pitch dictation progresses sequentially throughout *Celebrate Piano!™*. At first, the student writes one additional note. Eventually the student will write three or more notes before combining pitch and rhythm in melodic dictation. This ear skill develops aural awareness and supports excellent reading and performance. The steps for this activity may include:

- Play a pitch and go up a 2nd without the student watching
- Repeat and have the student sing the pitch and the 2nd
- Repeat again, and have the student draw a note with a stem on the appropriate line or space

Creativity

Question and Answer

The Question and Answer activity is introduced in Unit 6 with two-measure phrases. Play a two-measure Question (ending on a note other than Middle C), and ask the student to improvise a two-measure Answer that ends on C. Any Answer that ends on C and that matches the Question rhythmically is acceptable. Two sample Questions are provided in the *Lesson and Musicianship* book.

Question and Answer activities continue throughout Levels 1B, 2, 3, and 4. Eventually the student writes both the Question and the Answer, leading to the composition of short pieces by the end of *Celebrate Piano!™*.

Old MacDonald (p. 73)

The accompaniment for *Old MacDonald* is presented in two versions on both the MIDI disk and the CD. The first version represents the piece as printed in the *Lesson and Musicianship* book. The second version includes the entire piece so that the student can experience an accompaniment while they play the rest of the song by ear. Both versions appear under a single track listing.

LEVEL 1—UNIT 7: PLANNING FOR PREPARATION, PRESENTATION, AND FOLLOW-UP

Preparation
- Landmark C's
- Quarter rests
- Contrary motion

Presentation
- Staccato
- Time signatures: $\frac{2}{4}, \frac{3}{4}, \frac{4}{4}, \frac{6}{8}$
- Rhythmic dictation
- Stem direction

Follow-up
- Combining 2nds and 3rds
- Music alphabet
- Repeated patterns
- Letter clefs
- Quarter, half, dotted half, and whole notes
- HT
- 1, 2, 3, 4

UNIT 7: OVERVIEW

PAGE	ACTIVITY	PRESENTATION	PREPARATION ▲	SPECIAL ACTIVITY	DIV.
	Repertoire				
3	*The Grand Canyon*			Transpose	1
6	*Chinese Market*	Staccato		YBTJ!	1
9	*Duck Feet*	Time signature; staccato		Transpose	1
11	*Skating*	Time signature		YBTJ!	2
16	*Little Brown Jug*	Time signature			2
	Solos				
14	*Wake-up Dance*	Time signature; staccato			1
16	*The Whistle Song*	Time signature; staccato			2
	Finger Gyms				
4	*Staccato 2nds and 3rds*	Staccato		Transpose	1
10	*Fingers Together*		Landmarks; contrary motion		2
	Musicianship				
10	*Interval Stem-pede*	Stem direction			1
12	*Word Search*				2
	Rhythm				
8	*Clap and Count*	Time signature			2
13	*Just in Time*	Time signature			2
	Ear Skills				
5	*Interval Safari*				1
13	*Writing the Rhythms*	Rhythmic dictation			2
14	*Echo Game—Clapbacks!*		Rests		1
14	*Echo Game—Playbacks!*				2
	Creativity				
14	*Question and Answer*				2
15	*Sailing the C's*		Landmark C's		1

LEVEL 1—UNIT 7: INTEGRATED MUSICIANSHIP AND POSSIBLE SEQUENCE

Div. 1		**Div. 2**	
5	*Interval Safari*	14	*Echo Game—Playbacks!*
3	*The Grand Canyon*	14	*Question and Answer*
10	*Interval Stem-pede*	13	*Writing the Rhythms*
4	*Staccato 2nds and 3rds*	13	*Just in Time*
6	*Chinese Market*	16—Solos 1	*The Whistle Song*
14	*Echo Game—Clapbacks!*	10	*Fingers Together*
8	*Clap and Count*	11	*Skating*
9	*Duck Feet*	16	*Little Brown Jug*
14—Solos 1	*Wake-up Dance*	12	*Word Search*
15	*Sailing the C's*		

TEACHER'S NOTES AND TIPS

Musicianship

Time signatures are presented as $\frac{2}{4}$, $\frac{3}{4}$, $\frac{4}{4}$ and $\frac{6}{8}$ in order to reinforce the student's understanding of the quarter note as the basic unit of the beat note or ta. This approach also avoids confusion with fractions for young students. Students are still encouraged to tap and ta before they play; however, teachers may want to alternate ta counting with numeric counting. Counting numerically is useful in pieces where hands together playing is more involved.

Enrichment activity

Have the student go back and add time signatures to their favorite pieces.

Writing the Rhythms (p. 13) is the first rhythmic dictation. The steps for this activity may include:

• Clap or play a rhythm and have the student clap it back
• Repeat, and have the student clap and ta the rhythm. It helps to ask the student to say the rhythms aloud before notating.
• Have the student write the rhythm

These exercises become increasingly difficult throughout *Celebrate Piano!*™.

Technique

Staccato

Teachers should model a good wrist staccato for the student. A wrist staccato requires two motions: down and up. The student lifts the entire hand at the wrist while the forearm remains still and relaxed.

Tips:

Grand Canyon (p. 3) includes a review of many of the elements learned in Level 1A including dynamics, phrasing, 2nds and 3rds, rhythms, and HT playing.

Skating (p. 12) provides an opportunity to review legato and prepares contrary motion. It also reinforces playing HT with coordinated fingers.

LEVEL 1—UNIT 8: PLANNING FOR PREPARATION, PRESENTATION, AND FOLLOW-UP

Preparation
- Contrary motion
- 5ths
- Fingers 3–5
- Quarter and half rests

Presentation
- Independent fingers 1, 2, 3, 4, 5
- Grand staff: Treble and Bass clefs
- Landmarks: Treble C, Middle C, Bass C

Follow-up
- Combining 2nds and 3rds
- Quarter, half, dotted half, whole note
- Time signature
- 1, 2, 3, 4; 1–3; 2–4
- Staccato

UNIT 8: OVERVIEW

PAGE	ACTIVITY	PRESENTATION	PREPARATION ▲	SPECIAL ACTIVITY	DIV.
	Repertoire				
20	*Martian Madness*	Landmark C's		Transpose	1
21	*Bounce High, Bounce Low*	Middle C			1
22	*C Scherzo*	Treble and Bass C		YBTJ!	1
24	*Sammy C Serpent*	Treble and Bass C		Transpose	2
29	*Au claire de la lune*	Treble and Middle C	.	Transpose	2
	Solos				
17	*Sí,C, Señor*	Treble, Middle, Bass C's			2
	Finger Gyms				
17	*5-finger Aerobics*	Ind. fingers 1, 2, 3, 4, 5	Contrary motion; 5ths		1
19	*Interval Magic*	Grand staff; Treble and Bass C's	Contrary motion; fingers 3–5	Transpose; F9	2
	Musicianship				
18	*Grand staff; Treble clef and Bass clef*	Grand staff; landmark C's			2
19	*Landmark Detective*	Landmark C's		F8	1
25	*Lucy Locket*	Treble C		Transpose	2
25	*Interval Games*				1
26	*Sketching Clefs*	Treble and Bass clefs; Grand staff			2
	Rhythm				
26	*Just in Time*				1
	Ear Skills				
17	*Interval Safari*				1
27	*Writing the Notes*				2
27	*Echo Game—Clapbacks!*		Half rest		1
27	*Echo Game—Playbacks!*		Quarter rest		2
28	*Writing the Rhythms*				1
	Creativity				
28	*Question and Answer*				2
28	*The Spinning Top*				1

LEVEL 1—UNIT 8: INTEGRATED MUSICIANSHIP AND POSSIBLE SEQUENCE

Div. 1		Div. 2	
27	Echo Game—Clapbacks!	24	Sammy C Serpent
17	5-finger Aerobics	26	Sketching Clefs
26	Just in Time	19	Interval Magic
28	Writing the Rhythms	17—Solos 1	Sí, C, Señor
19	Landmark Detective	29	Au claire de la lune
20	Martian Madness	25	Lucy Locket
21	Bounce High, Bounce Low	28	Question and Answer
17	Interval Safari	27	Writing the Notes
25	Interval Games	27	Echo Game—Playbacks!
22	C Scherzo		
28	The Spinning Top		

TEACHER'S NOTES AND TIPS

Musicianship

Grand Staff; Landmark C's

The introduction of the Grand staff, Treble and Bass clefs, and the Landmark C's (Treble C, Middle C, and Bass C) is an important step for students as they begin to combine intervallic reading with landmarks. Students learn how to find their hand position without reference to a letter clef or keyboard chart by identifying the starting landmark. They can then continue to read interval direction and size.

Note that Middle C is shown for both the RH and LH—as it appears in actual music—rather than in the middle of the staff.

Flashcards

Flashcards provide reinforcement and drills for naming landmarks and reading intervals. When the skill of naming the note by first naming the landmark is secure, students can begin naming notes by imagining the landmark and naming the note. After the note has been named have the student play it on the keyboard.

Transposition

As intervallic and landmark reading continues, students play in multiple keys by transposing their pieces or activities to many different positions. (The concept of key and key signature is presented in Level 2.)

The ability to read intervals and to move to a wide variety of hand positions solidifies reading and leads students to experience a wide topography and a variety of keys.

Tips:

Students should now be quite efficient at naming the interval direction and size (start, up a 2nd, down a 3rd etc.). They must also relate this information to finger numbers. Students should "air play" each piece or play it on the closed keyboard cover using the correct fingers as they name the interval direction and size. This activity enhances the ability to transpose to a variety of hand positions.

Interval Games (p. 25) is an activity that teachers can do with their students on or off the bench. Have the students close their eyes as you call out intervals. It is fun for them to go through the game as fast as possible in order to name the final note! Intervallic reading becomes more secure as students learn to visualize keys and intervals quickly. Teachers and parents are encouraged to invent new games to challenge the student.

Sammy C Serpent (p. 24) and *Au claire de la lune* (p. 29) are excellent examples of pieces that engage the imagination. Be sure to discuss the title and illustration before playing.

Technique

Interval Magic (p. 19) is the first example of HT playing where the two hands are playing different rhythms—the RH moves to another finger while the LH stays in place. The student should be encouraged to tap the rhythms with the correct finger numbers on the keyboard cover before playing. The first time this appears in the repertoire is on p. 29, *Au claire de la lune*.

Ask your student to find the secret of playing HT with coordinated fingers: when the hands play together the same finger is used in each hand. This coordination provides physical security and ease as well as reading security.

Movement

Have your student create a dance to illustrate the intervals, phrases, and articulation in the repertoire. For example, the student may create a hopscotch pattern by hopping in place with feet close together on each harmonic 2nd, and feet wider apart on harmonic 3rds. For example, *C Scherzo* (p. 22):

- In m. 1, hop with feet close together on beat 1, hop with feet farther apart on beat 2, and hop with feet close again on beat 3.

- In m. 2, hop with feet apart on beat 1 and hold through beats 2 and 3.
- In mm. 3–4, take small steps on the 2nds and paint a rainbow in the air with the LH to illustrate the two-measure phrase.
- Repeat these steps for mm. 5–8 and 9–12.
- In mm. 13–14, illustrate the staccatos by patting the right knee with the RH on the staccato notes in the Treble clef, and patting the left knee with the LH for the staccato notes in the Bass clef.
- In m. 15, hop with the feet apart and hold through beats 2 and 3.
- In m. 16, hop on the left foot and hold through beats 2 ands 3.

Encourage your students to have fun creating their own movements!

LEVEL 1—UNIT 9: PLANNING FOR PREPARATION, PRESENTATION, AND FOLLOW-UP

Preparation
- 5ths
- Contrary motion
- Landmarks: Treble G
- Tie
- 3–5
- 1–5

Presentation
- Quarter, half, and whole rests
- Ledger lines
- Contrary motion

Follow-up
- Grand staff
- Treble and Bass clefs
- Landmark C's
- 2nds and 3rds
- Quarter, half, dotted half, and whole notes
- Time signature
- 1, 2, 3, 4; 1–3; 2–4

UNIT 9: OVERVIEW

PAGE	ACTIVITY	PRESENTATION	PREPARATION ▲	SPECIAL ACTIVITY	DIV.
	Repertoire				
32	*Night in the Jungle*	Rests			1
33	*Scary Sounds*	Rests		Transpose	1
34	*Ta Ta Tango*	Ledger lines; rests		F11	1
37	*Tiptoe*	Contrary motion; rests		Create	2
38	*Au contraire*	Contrary motion; rests		YBTJ!	2
41	*Yankee Doodle*	Ledger lines; rests		Transpose	2
	Solos				
18	*Bat Dance*	Ledger lines; rests			1
	Finger Gyms				
30	*5-finger Aerobics*		Contrary motion; 5th; 3–5, 1–5	Transpose	1
36	*Magic Mirrors*	Contrary motion			2
	Musicianship				
36	*Name that Note*				1
39	*Landmarks*				2
	Rhythm				
31	*The Name Game*	Rests		F10	1
39	*Tapping Game*	Rests			2
	Ear Skills				
30	*Interval Safari*				1
39	*Writing the Notes*				2
40	*Echo Game—Clapbacks!*		Tie		1
40	*Echo Game—Playbacks!*		Treble G		2
	Creativity				
40	*Musical Chairs*				1

LEVEL 1—UNIT 9: INTEGRATED MUSICIANSHIP AND POSSIBLE SEQUENCE

Div. 1			Div. 2		
30		*5-finger Aerobics*	39		*Landmarks*
30		*Interval Safari*	39		*Writing the Notes*
36		*Name that Note*	36		*Magic Mirrors*
40		*Echo Game—Clapbacks!*	37		*Tiptoe*
31		*The Name Game*	39		*Tapping Game*
32		*Night in the Jungle*	38		*Au contraire*
33		*Scary Sounds*	41		*Yankee Doodle*
34		*Ta Ta Tango*	40		*Echo Game—Playbacks!*
18—Solos 1		*Bat Dance*			
40		*Musical Chairs*			

TEACHER'S NOTES AND TIPS

Rhythm

The introduction of quarter, half, and whole rests provides more options for the repertoire and demands careful counting from the student. As the student claps and ta's or counts a rhythm, the teacher should ensure that an overt motion is made on the rest. We recommend pulsing the rest in the air with the hands open (palms up). Whisper the "ta" to indicate that a rest has a definite beat that must be felt and counted.

Night in the Jungle (p. 32) is a fun, rhythmic piece that is chanted. It may be performed as an ensemble by the teacher and student, parent and student, or with a group divided into gorillas and monkeys. Be sure to have the students feel both the notes and the rests. Teachers beware! After a rousing monkey and gorilla chant, it may be hard to get your student back on the bench for a quiet activity!

Movement

To illustrate rests, students may walk a rhythmic pattern, pausing to observe a rest.
For example, *Ta Ta Tango* (p. 34):
• In m. 1, step forward with the right foot on beat 1; step forward with the left foot on beat 2; pause on beat 3; and step forward with the right foot on beat 4.
• Repeat this pattern for mm. 3, 5, 9, 11, and 13.
• In m. 2, step back with the left foot on beat 1 and close with the right foot on beat 3 of the whole note.
• Repeat this pattern for mm. 4, 7, 8, 10, 12, 15, and 16.
• In mm. 6 and 14, simply step forward on each quarter note (L, R, L, R).
Create your own walking pattern for other pieces with rests!

Technique

Magic Mirrors (p. 36) introduces contrary motion. Students already know the secret of playing HT with coordinated fingers: when the hands play together the same finger is used in each hand. Now, have them discover that although the fingering and rhythm is the same when playing HT in contrary motion, the notes are different! Encourage this type of awareness as you learn other contrary motion pieces such as *Tiptoe* (p. 37).

Creativity

Tiptoe (p. 37) and *Musical Chairs* (p. 40) involve variation. This is a very structured creative activity that encourages the student to change one or two notes or rests in each measure. Creating a simple variation is an important first step in stylistic and jazz improvisation. Success in developing improvisational skills occurs with small steps. Eventually the student will feel comfortable changing several notes as they play.

Tips:

On p. 28, ask the student to improvise several Answers that end on C before writing their favorite Answer. Remind the student to maintain a steady beat.

The "magic key" to *Au contraire* (p. 38) lies in having the student count carefully while tapping HT. Ask questions that lead the student to discover that in mm. 3 and 5, the hands play together on beat 1 using the same finger number.

LEVEL 1—UNIT 10: PLANNING FOR PREPARATION, PRESENTATION, AND FOLLOW-UP

Preparation
- 5ths
- Half steps
- Sharps and flats
- Tie

Presentation
- Treble G
- Bass F
- 5ths
- 1–5

Follow-up
- Grand staff
- Treble and Bass clefs
- Landmark C's
- Ledger lines
- 2nds and 3rds
- Quarter, half, dotted half, and whole notes
- Rests: quarter, half, whole
- Time signature
- 1, 2, 3, 4; 1–3; 2–4

UNIT 10: OVERVIEW

PAGE	ACTIVITY	PRESENTATION	PREPARATION ▲	SPECIAL ACTIVITY	DIV.
	Repertoire				
44	*Happy Hiccups*	Treble G, Bass F			1
47	*Fuzzy Wuzzy*	Mel. and har. 5ths; 1–5; Treble G		Transpose	1
48	*Robot March*	Har. 5ths		YBTJ!	1
50	*Lyric Prelude*	5ths; Bass F		YBTJ!	2
55	*Bells in the Steeple*	5ths, Bass F		Create	2
	Solos				
21	*Highland Fling*	Treble G, Bass F			1
22	*Trumpet Parade*	5ths; Treble G, Bass F			2
	Finger Gyms				
42	*5-finger Warm-up*		5ths; 1–5	Transpose	1
51	*Interval Warm-up*	5ths; Treble G		Transpose	2
	Musicianship				
43	*Landmark Guide*	Treble G, Bass F		F12, F13	1
45	*Discovering 5ths*	Mel. and har. 5ths; 1–5		F14	1
46	*Landmark Map*	Treble G, Bass F			1
51	*Landmarks and their Neighbors*	5ths; Treble G, Bass F			2
51	*Name that Note*	Treble G, Bass F			2
52	*Close Companions*		Half steps; sharps and flats		2
	Rhythm				
52	*Rhythm Math Game*				1
53	*Rhythm Map*				2
	Ear Skills				
42	*Interval Safari*				1
46	*Interval Safari: Owl Song*	5ths			1
53	*Writing the Rhythms*				2
54	*Echo Game—Clapbacks!*		Tie		2
54	*Echo Game—Playbacks!*				2
	Creativity				
54	*Question and Answer*				2

LEVEL 1—UNIT 10: INTEGRATED MUSICIANSHIP AND POSSIBLE SEQUENCE

Div. 1			Div. 2		
42		*5-finger Warm-up*	51		*Interval Warm-up*
52		*Rhythm Math Game*	51		*Landmarks and Their*
43		*Landmark Guide*			*Neighbors*
46		*Landmark Map*	51		*Name that Note*
44		*Happy Hiccups*	50		*Lyric Prelude*
21—Solos 1		*Highland Fling*	55		*Bells in the Steeple*
42		*Interval Safari*	54		*Echo Game—Clapbacks!*
45		*Discovering 5ths*	53		*Writing the Rhythms*
46		*Interval Safari: Owl Song*	53		*Rhythm Map*
47		*Fuzzy Wuzzy*	54		*Echo Game—Playbacks!*
48		*Robot March*	54		*Question and Answer*
			22—Solos 1		*Trumpet Parade*
			52		*Close Companions*

TEACHER'S NOTES AND TIPS

Musicianship

Landmarks: Treble G and Bass F

By now, students should recognize the Landmark C's and be able to visualize and name the notes a 2nd or 3rd away from each landmark. The introduction of Treble G and Bass F gives the student a new set of landmarks within the Grand Staff. Teachers will need to spend ample time introducing these landmarks and having the student name the notes a 2nd and 3rd away from them.

Interval: 5th

The introduction of the 5th is the next step in intervallic reading. Students need to recognize that 5ths skip from a space to a space, skipping a space, or from a line to a line, skipping a line, and that 5ths are played with fingers 1 and 5. The *Owl Song* (p. 46) is the Interval Safari Song for the 5th.

Counting

As students encounter more HT playing, as in *Lyric Prelude* (p. 50), they should ta carefully, to reinforce the steady beat and count numerically, to recognize beat placement within each measure.

Technique

The parallel moving 5ths in *Robot March* (p. 48) should be played with a relaxed hand position. Be sure your student avoids a tense blocked 5th in either hand, as tension makes it difficult to move freely. Model a good wrist staccato with a relaxed wrist and forearm for your student. The student should be comfortable with this technique before going home to practice. Encourage the student to practice the moving 5ths without looking.

Tips:

Lyric Prelude (p. 50) is a beautiful legato piece in a cantabile style. Focus on shaping the legato phrases and ending each phrase softly.

Close Companions (p. 52) is a preparation activity for half and whole steps as well as sharps and flats. Teachers should help the student focus on the very next key up or down, without discussing half steps, whole steps, flats, or sharps.

LEVEL 1—UNIT 11: PLANNING FOR PREPARATION, PRESENTATION, AND FOLLOW-UP

Preparation
- 5-finger pattern
- Starting a 2nd or 3rd away from a landmark
- 4ths

Presentation
- Tie
- Flat, sharp, natural

Follow-up
- Landmarks: Treble G, Bass F, and C's
- 5ths, 2nds, 3rds
- Rests: quarter, half, whole

UNIT 11: OVERVIEW

PAGE	ACTIVITY	PRESENTATION	PREPARATION ▲	SPECIAL ACTIVITY	DIV.
	Repertoire				
57	Row, Row, Row Your Boat	Tie		F15; Transpose	1
59	Love Somebody	Flat		Transpose	1
61	Iggy Inchworm	Sharp, tie		YBTJ!	2
63	Mosquito Dance	Natural, sharp		Create	2
68	The Sad Dragon	Sharp, flat, tie		YBTJ!	2
	Solos				
24	A Quiet Moment				1
26	Ladybug Waltz	Sharp			2
	Finger Gyms				
56	5-finger Warm-up		5-finger pattern	Transpose	1
64	Four Score		4th	Transpose	2
	Musicianship				
58	Discovering Flats	Flats			1
58	Flat It!	Flats			1
58	Matching Game	Flats	Starting off landmarks		1
60	Discovering Sharps	Sharps			2
60	Sharp It!	Sharps			2
60	Matching Game	Sharps	Starting off landmarks		2
62	Twister	Sharp, flat, natural		F16	2
62	Melody Mechanics	Sharp, flat, natural, tie			2
64	Sign to the Left	Sharp, flat, natural			2
65	A-Mazing	Sharps and flats			2
	Rhythm				
66	Tie 'em Up	Tie			1
	Ear Skills				
56	Interval Safari				1
66	Writing the Notes				1
67	Echo Game—Clapbacks!				1
67	Echo Game—Playbacks!				2
	Creativity				
67	Question and Answer				1

LEVEL 1—UNIT 11: INTEGRATED MUSICIANSHIP AND POSSIBLE SEQUENCE

Div. 1			Div. 2		
24—Solos 1	*A Quiet Moment*		60	*Discovering Sharps*	
67	*Echo Game—Clapbacks!*		60	*Matching Game*	
57	*Row, Row, Row Your Boat*		60	*Sharp It!*	
66	*Tie 'em Up*		61	*Iggy Inchworm*	
56	*Interval Safari*		26—Solos 1	*Ladybug Waltz*	
56	*5-finger Warm-up*		62	*Twister*	
67	*Question and Answer*		64	*Four Score*	
66	*Writing the Notes*		63	*Mosquito Dance*	
58	*Discovering Flats*		62	*Melody Mechanics*	
58	*Matching Game*		64	*Sign to the Left*	
58	*Flat It!*		68	*The Sad Dragon*	
59	*Love Somebody*		65	*A-Mazing*	
			67	*Echo Game—Playbacks!*	

TEACHER'S NOTES AND TIPS

Musicianship

Sharps, flats, and naturals are presented in Unit 11. The "accidental rule," dealing with accidentals and bar lines, is presented on p. 62 without being named, since students are not familiar with the term accidental. Activities on pp. 62 and 64 emphasize writing the sharp or flat before the note.

Interval Safari

With the addition of the interval of a 5th in Unit 10, the student is ready to expand the interval game. The teacher or parent should play 2nds, 3rds, or 5ths and ask the student to name the interval played. (The student should not be able to see the keyboard.) Mix up the intervals and include both melodic and harmonic intervals. Begin from Middle C before moving to other places on the keyboard as the student becomes more secure.

Rhythm

There are two options for counting ties:
"Ta-tie" which clearly defines the tie.
"Ta-ah" which equates the tie with a half note.
Either system will correctly interpret the tie.

Tips:
Students typically have a hard time remembering which way a sharp or flat changes the pitch. Here is a fun way to help students remember:
- If a tire on a car goes flat, which way does it go? Answer: down.
- If you sit on a sharp tack, which way do you go? Answer: up!

Four Score (p. 64) is a preparation activity notated "off-staff" because students have not learned the interval of a 4th. Teachers should emphasize the hand position and fingering. Most students anticipate the 4ths and are pleased that they know what interval comes next!

The Sad Dragon (p. 68) provides another opportunity for dual counting. Ask the student to ta and play each hand separately and then to count and play HT. Highlight mm. 5 and 8 where one hand stays in place while the other hand moves.

LEVEL 1—UNIT 12: PLANNING FOR PREPARATION, PRESENTATION, AND FOLLOW-UP

Preparation
- 5-finger pattern
- Upbeat
- Starting away from landmarks

Presentation
- Interval: 4th—melodic and harmonic
- Time signatures: $\frac{2}{4}$, $\frac{3}{4}$, $\frac{4}{4}$
- 1–4, 2–5

Follow-up
- Sharps, flats, naturals
- Landmarks
- 2nd, 3rd, 5th
- Tie
- Quarter, half, and whole rests

UNIT 12: OVERVIEW

PAGE	ACTIVITY	PRESENTATION	PREPARATION ▲	SPECIAL ACTIVITY	DIV.
	Repertoire				
73	Aura Lee	Time signature; mel. 4ths		Transpose	1
74	Hoedown	Time signature; har. and mel. 4ths			1
75	Lazy Summer Day	Time signature; mel. 4ths		YBTJ!	2
78	Bravo!	Time signature; 4ths			2
	Solos				
28	The Teeter-Totter	Time signature; mel. 4ths			1
30	Crosswalk Parade	Time signature; mel. and har. 4ths			2
	Finger Gyms				
70	5-finger Tryout		5-finger pattern	Transpose	2
76	4th and 5th Dimension	Time signature; har. 4ths	5-finger pattern	Transpose	1
	Musicianship				
71	Discovering 4ths	Mel. and har. 4ths; 1–4; 2–5		F17	1
76	Who am I?		Starting off Landmarks		1
76	Writing Intervals	4ths			2
	Rhythm				
72	Time Travel	Time signature			1
	Ear Skills				
77	Writing the Rhythms	Time signature			2
70	Interval Safari				1
72	Interval Safari: Kangaroo Song	4ths			1
77	Echo Game—Clapbacks!		Upbeat		2
77	Echo Game—Playbacks!		5-finger pattern		1
	Creativity				
77	Question and Answer				1

LEVEL 1—UNIT 12: INTEGRATED MUSICIANSHIP AND POSSIBLE SEQUENCE

Div. 1			Div. 2		
76		*Who Am I?*	70		*5-finger Tryout*
70		*Interval Safari*	76		*Writing Intervals*
77		*Echo Game—Playbacks!*	75		*Lazy Summer Day*
77		*Question and Answer*	77		*Echo Game—Clapbacks!*
71		*Discovering 4ths*	77		*Writing the Rhythms*
72		*Interval Safari: Kangaroo Song*	78		*Bravo!*
72		*Time Travel*	76		*4th and 5th Dimension*
73		*Aura Lee*	30—Solos 1		*Crosswalk Parade*
28—Solos 1		*The Teeter-Totter*			
76		*4th and 5th Dimension*			
74		*Hoedown*			

TEACHER'S NOTES AND TIPS

Musicianship

Interval: 4th

The introduction of the 4th is the next step in intervallic reading. Students need to recognize that 4ths skip from a space to a line, or from a line to a line to a space, and that 4ths are played with either fingers 1–4 or 2–5.

The *Kangaroo Song* is the Interval Safari song for the 4th. The teacher may now expand the Interval Safari to include 4ths. The teacher or parent should play 2nds, 3rds, 4ths, or 5ths and ask the student to name the interval played. (The student should not be able to see the keyboard.) Mix up the intervals and include both melodic and harmonic intervals.

Movement

Create your own partner dance for *Hoedown* (p. 74) to reinforce the echoing (call and response) 4ths and contrary motion.

- In mm. 1 and 5, the first person (student), or group, hops in place on beats 1 and 2 with feet spread to shoulder width to represent 4ths. The second person (teacher), or group, hops in place on beats 3 and 4 (the response).

- Repeat for mm. 2 and 6, hopping only once on the half notes.
- In mm. 3 and 7, both partners step forward towards each other on each quarter note beat.
- In mm. 4 and 8, give each other a salute on beat 1 and step backward on beats 2 and 3.

Technique

Notice that the HT fingering on *Hoedown* (p. 74) and *Lazy Summer Day* (p. 75) is still carefully coordinated so that the same fingers play in each hand for ease of reading. *Aura Lee* (p. 73) uses some non-coordinated fingering in preparation for pieces with more difficult independent fingering and contrapuntal lines.

Tips:

5-finger Tryout (p. 70) and *4th and 5th Dimension* (p. 76) prepare for the 5-finger pattern that will be introduced in Level 2A.

Bravo! (p. 78) is a rich, full-sounding piece which reviews many of the concepts presented in Level 1, including intervals, rhythms, and dynamics.

Level 2

SCOPE AND SEQUENCE

UNIT	MUSICIANSHIP/READING	RHYTHM	TECHNIQUE	EAR SKILLS	CREATIVITY
LEVEL 2A					
1	• Review landmarks: Treble C, Middle C, Bass C, Bass F, Treble G • Review 2nds, 3rds, 4ths, 5ths • Landmarks: High C, Low C • Review ledger lines • Half and whole step			• Review 2nds, 3rds, 4ths, 5ths	• Question and Answer
2	• Starting a 2nd or 3rd away from a landmark • *pp, ff*			• Rhythmic dictation	• Variation • Composition
3	• Major 5-finger patterns starting on white keys • Tonic and Dominant—single note accompaniment	• Upbeat or pickup	• 5-finger pattern	• Pattern recognition	• Question and Answer: ending on Tonic • Composition
4	• Starting a 4th or 5th away from a landmark	• Eighth notes		• Pitch dictation	• Question and Answer: ending on Tonic
5	• Interval: 6th • 5th–6th–5th accompaniment • Accent • Major 5-finger patterns starting on black keys		• 5-finger pattern • 5th–6th–5th	• 6th • 5th–6th–5th • Pitch dictation	• Variation • Question and Answer
6	• Key signatures: sharp keys	• Eighth rest		• Eighth notes	• Question and Answer • Composition
LEVEL 2B					
7	• *Crescendo, diminuendo* • Major triads	• Dotted quarter	• Major triads blocked and broken	• Add missing sounds to 5- or 6-note melodies	• Question and Answer: parallel and contrasting
8	• Octave • Key signatures: flat keys	• Fermata	• Octave	• Octave • Solfège • Mystery melody	• Improvisation
9	• Ostinato	• *Ritardando* • Tempo, *a tempo*	• Staccato vs. legato	• Identify patterns	• Question and Answer: parallel and contrasting • Improvisation
10	• 7th • Form: AB, ABA • *D.C. al Fine*		• 7ths	• 7th • Rhythmic dictation	• Variation
11	• Form: Introduction, *Coda* • 8va	• Upbeat—eighth note	• Finger crossing	• Mystery melody	• Question and Answer: parallel and contrasting
12	• *mf, mp*	• Common time: C		• Pitch dictation	• Question and Answer • Variation

LEVEL 2—UNIT 1: PLANNING FOR PREPARATION, PRESENTATION, AND FOLLOW-UP

Preparation
- 5-finger pattern
- Starting a 2nd or 3rd away from landmarks
- 1–5–1
- Parallel motion
- *pp* and *ff*

Presentation
- Landmarks: High C, Low C
- Half and whole steps

Follow-up
- Review 2nds, 3rds, 4ths, 5ths
- Quarter, half, dotted half, whole
- Ledger lines

UNIT 1: OVERVIEW

PAGE	ACTIVITY	PRESENTATION	PREPARATION ▲	SPECIAL ACTIVITY	DIV.
	Repertoire				
7	*Circus Tumblers*				1
9	*Unlikely Friends*	High C, Low C			1
10	*Secret Agent*	High C, Low C		YBTJ!	2
11	*Allegro*			Transpose	2
	Solos				
5	*Flying High*				1
6	*Rain on the Pagoda*	High C, Low C			2
	Finger Gyms				
5	*Staccato Dance*		5-finger pattern		1
13	*Hidden Half Steps*	Half and whole steps	5-finger pattern; parallel motion	Transpose	2
	Musicianship				
5	*Landmark Launch*				1
8	*Leaping Landmarks*	High C, Low C		F18	1
8	*Name that Note*	High C, Low C	Starting a 2nd or 3rd away from a landmark		1
12	*Half Step Hunt*	Half steps			2
12	*Whole Step Hunt*	Whole steps			2
13	*Disappearing Dinosaurs*	High C, Low C	*pp* and *ff*		1
14	*What Am I?*	High C, Low C			2
	Rhythm				
14	*Rest-ing Up*				1
15	*Math Game*				1
	Ear Skills				
6	*Interval Safari*				1
15	*Pattern Detective*				2
16	*Echo Game—Clapbacks!*				1
16	*Echo Game—Playbacks!*				2
	Creativity				
16	*Question and Answer*			Transpose	1
12	*Half Step Hula*				2

LEVEL 2—UNIT 1: INTEGRATED MUSICIANSHIP AND POSSIBLE SEQUENCE

Div. 1			Div. 2		
5		*Landmark Launch*	15		*Echo Game—Playbacks!*
6		*Interval Safari*	16		*Pattern Detective*
16		*Question and Answer*	12		*Half Step Hunt*
5		*Staccato Dance*	12		*Whole Step Hunt*
7		*Circus Tumblers*	12		*Half Step Hula*
14		*Rest-ing Up*	13		*Hidden Half Steps*
15		*Math Game*	10		*Secret Agent*
16		*Echo Game—Clapbacks!*	6	—Solos 2	*Rain on the Pagoda*
5	—Solos 2	*Flying High*	11		*Allegro*
8		*Leaping Landmarks*	14		*What am I?*
9		*Unlikely Friends*			
8		*Name that Note*			
13		*Disappearing Dinosaurs*			

TEACHER'S NOTES AND TIPS

Much of the material in Level 2, Unit 1 reviews the landmarks, intervals, rhythms, and other elements presented in Level 1. Continuing students as well as transfer students who may be entering *Celebrate Piano!*™ at this level should take the time to review these elements carefully.

Musicianship
Landmarks: High C and Low C
The landmarks High C and Low C are presented in this unit, expanding the reading range of the student. They will now be able to read from a 5th below Low C to a 5th above High C. Familiarity with the ledger lines above and below the Grand Staff will serve students well when they approach early classical music.

Continue to use Flashcards for frequent drill and reinforcement.

Half Steps and Whole Steps
Half steps and whole steps are presented in this unit in preparation for 5-finger patterns and scale formulas. Review sharps and flats by relating them to the half steps.

Continue to do quick drills to find half and whole steps, and sharps and flats on the piano.

T I P PS
Parents and teachers are encouraged to frequently review **T I P PS**—the steps for successful practicing—with the student.

Tips:
Unlikely Friends (p. 9): After playing the RH high C in m. 8, the student will need to look down quickly to locate the LH low C that follows.

Secret Agent (p. 10): How can the student make this music sound mysterious? Is the RH someone tipoeing quietly? Is the secret agent looking around for clues on each phrase and quietly moving on the staccatos?

Classical Repertoire
Allegro, by Daniel Gottlob Türk, is the first classical piece introduced to the student. Every effort has been made to present early or introductory level classical pieces that reinforce the concepts used in the method. The authors have made a commitment not to simplify, transpose, or otherwise alter original compositions by classical composers.

Türk included no phrasing or articulation marks in *Allegro*. Some teachers will choose to detach the quarter notes, while others may prefer a different approach. You may also experiment with phrasing (2+2+4 or 4+4). Have the student write in the articulation choices that you have discussed.

LEVEL 2—UNIT 2: PLANNING FOR PREPARATION, PRESENTATION, AND FOLLOW-UP

Preparation
- 5-finger pattern
- *pp* and *ff*
- Eighth notes

Presentation
- Starting a 2nd or 3rd away from a landmark
- *pp* and *ff*

Follow-up
- Half and whole steps
- Landmarks: High C, Low C
- Contrary motion

UNIT 2: OVERVIEW

PAGE	ACTIVITY	PRESENTATION	PREPARATION ▲	SPECIAL ACTIVITY	DIV.
19	**Repertoire** *Lightly Row*	Starting away from a landmark		Transpose	1
20	*Cheery Cello*	Starting away from a landmark		Transpose	1
21	*Blue-zy Blues*	*ff*; starting away from a landmark		YBTJ!	2
22	*Iroquois Lullaby*	*pp*; starting away from a landmark			2
7	**Solos** *Elephant Dance*	*ff*; starting away from a landmark			2
9	*Tilt-a-Whirl*	*pp*; starting away from a landmark			1
17	**Finger Gyms** *Stepping Stones*		5-finger pattern; *pp* and *ff*	Transpose	1
23	*Contrary Steps*	Starting away from a landmark	5-finger pattern	Transpose	2
18	**Musicianship** *Away from Home*	Starting away from a landmark		F19	1
23	*Grab Bag*	Starting away from a landmark			2
24	*Building Blocks*				1
25	**Rhythm** *Color by Rhythm*				2
17	**Ear Skills** *Interval Safari*				1
26	*Writing the Rhythm*				2
26	*Echo Game—Clapbacks!*		Eighth notes		2
26	*Echo Game—Playbacks!*		5-finger pattern; eighth notes		1
27	**Creativity** *Dynamic Variation*	*pp* and *ff*			2
27	*Iroquois Lullaby*				2

LEVEL 2—UNIT 2: INTEGRATED MUSICIANSHIP AND POSSIBLE SEQUENCE

Div. 1			Div. 2		
26	*Echo Game—Playbacks!*		26	*Echo Game—Clapbacks!*	
17	*Stepping Stones*		25	*Color by Rhythm*	
24	*Building Blocks*		26	*Writing the Rhythm*	
17	*Interval Safari*		21	*Blue-zy Blues*	
18	*Away from Home*		7—Solos 2	*Elephant Dance*	
19	*Lightly Row*		27	*Dynamic Variation*	
20	*Cheery Cello*		23	*Grab Bag*	
9—Solos 2	*Tilt-a-Whirl*		23	*Contrary Steps*	
			22	*Iroquois Lullaby*	
			27	*Iroquois Lullaby* (creative)	

TEACHER'S NOTES AND TIPS

Musicianship

Starting Away from Landmarks

Starting away from landmarks is the primary concept presented in this unit. Up to this point, students have always seen a landmark and then read intervals from that landmark. It may be a difficult transition for students to now imagine those landmarks, relate the direction and distance of the starting notes to those imaginary landmarks, and name the notes. This new skill will take much practice before the student is secure. Flashcards are one of the most effective practice tools for reinforcing this concept. Have students name the nearest landmark, determine the distance and direction between the two notes, and then name the note (Treble C, down a 3rd, A). As students become more secure, they should practice naming individual notes on the flashcards without first naming the landmark and the interval. Consistent practice will strengthen this new skill.

Ear Skills

Interval Safari

Students need to continually sing Middle C on pitch and to review the interval songs. Play an interval anywhere on the keyboard for the student to identify (M2, M3, P4, P5). For singing, however, it is best for the student to relate the pitch to Middle C.

Writing the Rhythm (p. 26): Clap or play a pattern using quarter, half, dotted half, and whole notes or rests for the student to echo before writing. Stress the downbeat of each measure.

Movement

Students may continue to use large body movements to represent the elements of music. For each piece in the unit, the student may:

- Pat or tap the phrases with large forearm motions if the marking is *f* or *ff*; with smaller motions if the marking is *p* or *pp*
- March with a large (*f*) or small (*p*) motion from the knees in $\frac{2}{4}$ or $\frac{4}{4}$ meter
- Swing the arms in a semicircle, with a large (*f*) or small (*p*) motion, on beats 1–3 in triple meter

Tips:

Blue-zy Blues (p. 21): Notice the LH pattern with its unique fingering. Have the student play the LH quarter notes detached. Beats 2 and 4 may be accented to give *Blue-zy Blues* a traditional jazz feeling.

Iroquois Lullaby (p. 22): "Kiyokeena" is pronounced Ki (as in eye)–yo–kee–na.

LEVEL 2—UNIT 3: PLANNING FOR PREPARATION, PRESENTATION, AND FOLLOW-UP

Preparation
- Staccato vs. legato
- 5-finger pattern
- 6ths
- 5th–6th–5th
- Eighth notes

Presentation
- Upbeat or pickup
- Major 5-finger patterns: white keys
- Tonic, Dominant

Follow-up
- Half and whole steps
- High C, Low C
- *pp* and *ff*
- Starting away from landmarks

UNIT 3: OVERVIEW

PAGE	ACTIVITY	PRESENTATION	PREPARATION ▲	SPECIAL ACTIVITY	DIV.
	Repertoire				
30	*The Frantic Ant*	Upbeat			1
31	*Russian Winter*	Upbeat		YBTJ!	1
34	*Easy Day*	5-finger pattern; Tonic and Dominant		Transpose	2
36	*When the Saints Go Marching In*	Tonic and Dominant; 5-finger pattern; upbeat		Transpose	2
	Solos				
10	*Grasshoppers on Parade*	Upbeat; 5-finger pattern			1
13	*In a Little Spanish Village*	5-finger pattern; Tonic and Dominant			2
	Finger Gyms				
28	*5-finger Gymnastics*		5-finger pattern; staccato vs. legato	Transpose	1
32	*5-finger Warm-up*	5-finger pattern		Transpose	2
38	*Stretches*		6th; 5th–6th–5th	Transpose	2
	Musicianship				
32	*White-key Patterns*	5-finger pattern			2
33	*Touchdown*	Tonic and Dominant; 5-finger pattern			2
39	*Spelling Challenge*	5-finger pattern			2
40	*Imagine This*		6th		1
40	*Interval Madness*				1
	Rhythm				
29	*Upbeat Investigation*	Upbeat			1
	Ear Skills				
28	*Interval Safari*				1
41	*Pattern Detective*				2
41	*Echo Game—Clapbacks!*		Eighth notes		1
41	*Echo Game—Playbacks!*		Eighth notes		2
	Creativity				
42	*Question and Answer*				2
43	*Moving Melodies*				2

LEVEL 2—UNIT 3: INTEGRATED MUSICIANSHIP AND POSSIBLE SEQUENCE

Div. 1		Div. 2	
28	*Interval Safari*	28	Review *5-finger Gymnastics*
40	*Imagine This*	32	*White-key Patterns*
40	*Interval Madness*	32	*5-finger Warm-up*
28	*5-finger Gymnastics*	41	*Pattern Detective*
41	*Echo Game—Clapbacks!*	41	*Echo Game—Playbacks!*
29	*Upbeat Investigation*	39	*Spelling Challenge*
30	*The Frantic Ant*	33	*Touchdown*
31	*Russian Winter*	34	*Easy Day*
10—Solos 2	*Grasshoppers on Parade*	12—Solos 2	*In a Little Spanish Village*
		42	*Question and Answer*
		36	*When the Saints Go Marching In*
		43	*Moving Melodies*
		38	*Stretches*

TEACHER'S NOTES AND TIPS

Musicianship

Major 5-finger Patterns

The half- and whole-step *Magic Formula* for Major 5-finger patterns is presented in this unit. Students have been playing in these patterns and transposing to a wide variety of hand positions and 5-finger patterns since Level 1 using keyboard graphics or landmarks. This is the first time, however, that we define the formula of half steps and whole steps for the 5-finger pattern and ask students to recognize and name them. Students will need to memorize this formula and use it to find both white- and black-key patterns until they know them securely. The repertoire in this unit reinforces the white-key 5-finger patterns—C, D, E, F, G, A, and B major. Black-key patterns are presented in Unit 5.

Students are encouraged to review 5-finger patterns and transpose to new 5-finger patterns throughout Levels 2, 3, and 4. They are also asked to "warm up" in the pattern before they play as a means of reviewing the hand position.

Tonic and Dominant

Tonic and Dominant notes are also presented. This step forward in theory identifies the first and fifth notes of the 5-finger pattern (later of the key or scale), that are used to form accompaniment patterns. This is also preparation for the introduction of the I and V chords in Level 3.

Stretches (p. 38) prepares the student for the interval of a 6th. Since the 6th may be formed by expanding the 5th, students need to practice stretching up a whole step or down a half step to form the interval. This is preparation: simply help the student learn the exercise without naming the interval.

Rhythm

When presenting the upbeat, remember to teach the student how to "count in" before playing. They must recognize the time signature, number of beats in the incomplete measure, and adjust their count-in pattern. Decide whether to give a one- or two-measure preparation before playing. It is often easier to count two measures when beginning with an upbeat.

Creativity

On p. 42, the student is asked to create a four-measure Answer. Encourage the student to maintain a steady beat while improvising.

LEVEL 2—UNIT 4: PLANNING FOR PREPARATION, PRESENTATION, AND FOLLOW-UP

Preparation
- 6ths
- 5th–6th–5th
- Major triads
- Eighth rest

Presentation
- Starting a 4th or 5th away from a landmark
- Eighth notes
- Pitch dictation

Follow-up
- High C, Low C
- *pp* and *ff*
- Major white-key 5-finger patterns
- Tonic, Dominant
- Upbeat

UNIT 4: OVERVIEW

PAGE	ACTIVITY	PRESENTATION	PREPARATION ▲	SPECIAL ACTIVITY	DIV.
	Repertoire				
45	*The Lovable Ladybug*	Starting away from a landmark		Transpose	1
47	*Allegretto*	Eighth notes		Transpose	1
48	*Highland Tune*	Eighth notes; starting away from a landmark		YBTJ!	2
49	*Trumpets and Horns*	Eighth notes; starting away from a landmark			2
	Solos				
14	*Bouncing Balls*	Eighth notes			1
15	*The Mouse in the Grandfather Clock*	Eighth notes; starting away from a landmark			2
16	*Etude*	Eighth notes			2
	Finger Gyms				
50	*Quarters and Eighths*	Eighth notes		Transpose	1
50	*Stretch and Run*	Eighth notes	5th–6th–5th; 6th; triads		2
	Musicianship				
44	*Away from Home*	Starting a 4th or 5th away from a landmark		F20	1
51	*Missing Finger Numbers*				1
52	*Musical Word Search*				2
	Rhythm				
46	*Eighth Note Discovery*	Eighth notes		F21	1
	Ear Skills				
44	*Interval Safari*				1
51	*Echo Game—Clapbacks!*		Eighth rest		2
51	*Echo Game—Playbacks!*				1
54	*Pitch Detective*	Pitch dictation			2
	Creativity				
54	*Question and Answer*				2
54	*Whole Step Hustle*				1

LEVEL 2—UNIT 4: INTEGRATED MUSICIANSHIP AND POSSIBLE SEQUENCE

Div. 1		Div. 2	
51	*Missing Finger Numbers*	51	*Echo Game—Clapbacks!*
54	*Whole Step Hustle*	54	*Question and Answer*
44	*Interval Safari*	54	*Pitch Detective*
44	*Away from Home*	48	*Highland Tune*
45	*The Lovable Ladybug*	49	*Trumpets and Horns*
51	*Echo Game—Playbacks!*	50	*Stretch and Run*
46	*Eighth Note Discovery*	15—Solos 2	*The Mouse in the Grandfather Clock*
47	*Allegretto*		
50	*Quarters and Eighths*	52	*Musical Word Search*
14—Solos 2	*Bouncing Balls*	16—Solos 2	*Etude*

TEACHER'S NOTES AND TIPS

Musicianship

Unit 4 extends the reading skill of starting away from a landmark by including notes that are a 4th or 5th away. As in Unit 2, students must first imagine and identify the landmark that is closest to the given note, then name the direction and distance from the landmark before naming the note (Treble C, up a 4th, F, etc.). Continue to use Flashcards to reinforce this reading skill.

Rhythm

Eighth Notes

Eighth notes are presented in this unit and counted as "ti" (pronounced "tea"). In this unit, eighth notes are usually found in groups of two, joined with a beam. Eighth notes are contrasted with quarter notes and half notes.

Movement

Create a dance or movement pattern to help students feel different rhythmic values. Here are some ideas:
- Point the toe on each quarter note, and step-step on each group of two eighth notes
- Bend the knees on each quarter note and clap the eighth notes
- Stomp the quarter notes and snap the fingers on the eighth notes

Ear Skills

Pitch Detective (p. 54) has now expanded to include three notes. In order for the student to concentrate on pitch discrimination, it is important that the teacher play only quarter notes. Pitch and rhythmic dictation will be combined later in *Celebrate Piano!*™.

Begin with a simple pattern such as—Middle C, up a 2nd, down a 2nd—before moving to combinations like Middle C, up a 5th, down a 3rd.

Tip:

Teachers should explore several options for phrasing and articulation in *Allegretto* (p. 47).

LEVEL 2—UNIT 5: PLANNING FOR PREPARATION, PRESENTATION, AND FOLLOW-UP

Preparation
- Eighth rest
- Dotted quarter note
- Major triads
- *Crescendo*

Presentation
- Interval: 6th
- 5th–6th–5th accompaniments
- Accent
- Major 5-finger patterns: black keys

Follow-up
- Sharps, flats, and naturals
- Major white-key 5-finger patterns
- Tonic, Dominant
- Upbeat quarter note
- Eighth notes
- Pitch dictation

UNIT 5: OVERVIEW

PAGE	ACTIVITY	PRESENTATION	PREPARATION ▲	SPECIAL ACTIVITY	DIV.
	Repertoire				
58	*Lavender's Blue*	6th; 5th–6th–5th		Transpose	1
60	*Pop Goes the Weasel*	Accent; 6th; 5th–6th–5th		YBTJ!	2
61	*Proud Moment*	6th; 5th–6th–5th		Transpose	1
64	*Quiet as a Mouse*	5-finger patterns, black keys			2
	Solos				
17	*A Piece to Begin*				1
18	*Fiddlin' Around*	5-finger patterns, black keys			1
20	*Indian Dance*	6th; accent			2
	Finger Gyms				
55	*Finger Fitness*			Transpose	1
56	*Up, Down Boogie*	5th–6th–5th			2
57	*5th–6th–5th Shuffle*	5th–6th–5th		Transpose	1
76	*Fingers Together*		Triads; *crescendo*		2
	Musicianship				
56	*Discovering 6ths*	6th		F22	1
57	*Ride with Me*	5th–6th–5th		Transpose	1
62	*Black-key Patterns*	5-finger patterns, black keys		Transpose	2
62	*Intervals, Intervals, Intervals!*	6ths			1
63	*Spelling Challenge*	5-finger patterns, black keys			2
63	*Sharp, Natural, Flat Fun*				2
	Rhythm				
65	*Time Signature Workout*				2
	Ear Skills				
66	*Interval Safari: Elephant Song*	6th			1
66	*Pitch Detective*				2
67	*Echo Game—Clapbacks!*		Dotted quarter-eighth; eighth rest		2
67	*Echo Game—Playbacks!*				1
	Creativity				
59	*Lavender Variation*	5th–6th–5th			1
67	*Question and Answer*	5-finger patterns, black keys			2

LEVEL 2—UNIT 5: INTEGRATED MUSICIANSHIP AND POSSIBLE SEQUENCE

Div. 1			Div. 2		
55		*Finger Fitness*	60		*Pop Goes the Weasel*
17—Solos 2		*A Piece to Begin*	20—Solos 2		*Indian Dance*
67		*Echo Game—Playbacks!*	63		*Sharp, Natural, Flat Fun*
56		*Discovering 6ths*	67		*Question and Answer*
66		*Interval Safari: Elephant Song*	66		*Pitch Detective*
57		*5th–6th Shuffle*	62		*Black-key Patterns*
57		*Ride With Me*	62		*Up, Down Boogie*
58		*Lavender's Blue*	64		*Quiet as a Mouse*
59		*Lavender Variation*	63		*Spelling Challenge*
61		*Proud Moment*	67		*Echo Game—Clapbacks!*
62		*Intervals, Intervals, Intervals*	65		*Time Signature Workout*
18—Solos 2		*Fiddlin' Around*	65		*Fingers Together*

TEACHER'S NOTES AND TIPS

Several important concepts are introduced in Unit 5: the interval of a 6th; the 5th–6th–5th accompaniment figure; and 5-finger patterns starting on black keys.

Musicianship

5th–6th–5th Accompaniment Pattern
With the introduction of the 6th, students can now accompany with both 5ths and 6ths. *Up, Down Boogie* (p. 56) is a Finger Gym that can be used as a warm-up exercise for pieces that include a 5th–6th–5th accompaniment pattern. Point out that when moving up from a 5th to a 6th, there is a stretch of a whole step, while there is a stretch of only a half step when moving down from a 5th to a 6th (like the 5th–6th–5th accompaniment pattern).

After warming up with *Up Down Boogie*, discover the melodic and harmonic 6ths in *Lavender's Blue* (p. 58) and discuss the half and whole step stretch.

Ride with Me (p. 57) gives the student an opportunity to accompany a simple melody with the new 5th–6th–5th pattern and to transpose both melody and accompaniment. You may wish to challenge your students to transpose this piece to many different keys.

The introduction of the 5th–6th–5th accompaniment pattern starts to build an aural and physical sense of the I–V^7–I chord progression, which will be introduced in Level 3.

Finger Gyms

There are many different Finger Gym exercises in this unit, which reinforce the 5th–6th–5th accompaniment pattern, and the new black key 5-finger patterns. Several of these exercises also prepare the student for blocked and broken chords and are therefore presented with "off-staff" notation.

Creativity

The *Question and Answer* on p. 67 has expanded to four-measure phrases and asks the student to end on the Tonic or keynote. Encourage students to create several different answers and to accurately notate their favorite answer.

Tip:

Quiet as a Mouse presents a variety of challenges including the black key 5-finger patterns (D♭ and E♭ Major), legato vs. staccato touches, phrasing, and dynamics.

LEVEL 2—UNIT 6: PLANNING FOR PREPARATION, PRESENTATION, AND FOLLOW-UP

Preparation
- Major triads
- Dotted quarter note
- *Crescendo, diminuendo*

Presentation
- Key signatures: sharp keys
- Eighth rest

Follow-up
- All Major 5-finger patterns
- Tonic, Dominant
- Upbeat
- Accent
- 5th–6th–5th
- Eighth notes

UNIT 6: OVERVIEW

PAGE	ACTIVITY	PRESENTATION	PREPARATION ▲	SPECIAL ACTIVITY	DIV.
	Repertoire				
70	*In the Forest*	Key signatures		YBTJ!	1
72	*Whistle, Daughter, Whistle*	Key signatures		Transpose	1
73	*Run Around*	Key signatures		Transpose	2
79	*The Boogie Bugler*	Eighth rest; key signatures			2
	Solos				
21	*Clowns*				1
22	*Moonwalker March*	Key signatures			2
	Finger Gyms				
68	*5-finger Funtastics*		*Crescendo*	Transpose	1
74	*More Fingers Together*		Major triads; *Diminuendo*	Transpose	2
	Musicianship				
69	*Key Signature Hunt*	Key signatures: sharp keys		F23	1
74	*Naming the Keys*	Key signatures			1
75	*Tracing Sharps*	Key signatures			2
75	*Key Signature Challenge*	Key signatures			2
76	*Reading Melodies*	Eighth rest; key signatures			2
	Rhythm				
76	*Resting Eighths*	Eighth rest		F24	2
	Ear Skills				
68	*Interval Safari*				1
77	*Pattern Detective*				2
77	*Echo Game—Clapbacks!*	Eighth rest	Dotted quarter-eighth		2
77	*Echo Game—Playbacks!*				1
	Creativity				
78	*Question and Answer*	Key signatures			1
78	*Rhythm Swap*			Transpose	2

LEVEL 2—UNIT 6: INTEGRATED MUSICIANSHIP AND POSSIBLE SEQUENCE

Div. 1

68	*Interval Safari*
21—Solos 2	*Clowns*
68	*5-finger Funtastics*
77	*Echo Game—Playbacks!*
69	*Key Signature Hunt*
70	*In the Forest*
72	*Whistle, Daughter, Whistle*
78	*Question and Answer*
74	*Naming the Keys*

Div. 2

75	*Tracing Sharps*
75	*Key Signature Challenge*
73	*Run Around*
22—Solos 2	*Moonwalker March*
77	*Echo Game—Clapbacks!*
76	*Resting Eighths*
76	*Reading Melodies*
77	*Pattern Detective*
79	*The Boogie Bugler*
74	*More Fingers Together*
78	*Rhythm Swap*

TEACHER'S NOTES AND TIPS

Musicianship
Sharp Keys

Unit 6 introduces key signatures for sharp keys and contains repertoire in the keys of G, D, A, and E Major, with activities and transposition to many other keys. Only the notated key signature is new in this unit. Students have been playing in Major 5-finger patterns since Unit 2 of Level 2 and have been playing and transposing in multiple keys since Level 1, which eases the transition to reading the key signature and remembering sharps.

When presenting key signatures at this stage, we do not refer to the scale but to a "key family." The student has learned the 5-finger patterns for all twelve keys but has not yet experienced a full scale.

When naming sharp key signatures, ask the student to name the last sharp and then go up a half step to name the key. They should always include the sharp in the name or they will be confused on both C♯ and F♯ Major (B♯ up a half step is C♯, not C).

Flashcards (F23): Have the student name the key signature, then quickly find the corresponding hand position HT on the keyboard.

Rhythm
Eighth Rest

The eighth rest is presented in this unit. Students should be encouraged to whisper "ti" or "rest" for the rest as they pulse the beat.

Creativity

Rhythm Swap (p. 78): Encourage the student to clap and chant the rhythm, then choose a starting pitch before improvising a melody.

LEVEL 2—UNIT 7: PLANNING FOR PREPARATION, PRESENTATION, AND FOLLOW-UP

Preparation
- Staccato vs. legato
- Octave

Presentation
- Dotted quarter note
- Dotted quarter-eighth notes
- Major triads
- *Crescendo, diminuendo*
- Question and Answer: parallel and contrasting answers

Follow-up
- Tonic
- All Major 5-finger patterns
- Key signatures: sharp keys
- Eighth notes and rests
- Upbeat quarter note
- 5th–6th–5th
- 6th

UNIT 7: OVERVIEW

PAGE	ACTIVITY	PRESENTATION	PREPARATION ▲	SPECIAL ACTIVITY	DIV.
	Repertoire				
4	*Rockin' Sunrise*				1
7	*Exotic Birds*	Dotted quarter-eighth note		Transpose	1
9	*Triadic Triumph*	Major triad			2
10	*The Parade*	*Cresc., dim.*; Major triad; dotted quarter-eighth note		YBTJ!	2
16	*The Hound Dawg Song*	Major triads; dotted quarter-eighth note		Transpose	2
	Solos				
25	*Fanfare*				2
27	*Let's Waltz*	*Dim.*			1
28	*Little Song*	*Cresc.*			1
	Finger Gyms				
5	*Banjo and Cello— Imagine That!*		Staccato vs. legato	Transpose	1
8	*Broken and Blocked Triads*	Blocked and broken triads		Transpose	2
12	*Rainbow Leaps*		Octave		2
	Musicianship				
8	*Discovering Triads*	Major triad		F25	2
12	*Triple Treat*	Major triad			2
13	*Coded Message*				1
	Rhythm				
6	*Dotted Quarter Discovery*	Dotted quarter-eighth note		F26	1
	Ear Skills				
5	*Interval Safari*				1
14	*Pitch Detective*				1
14	*Echo Game Clapbacks!*	Dotted quarter-eighth note			1
14	*Echo Game—Playbacks!*	Dotted quarter-eighth note			2
	Creativity				
15	*Question and Answer*	Parallel and contrasting Answers			2

LEVEL 2—UNIT 7: INTEGRATED MUSICIANSHIP AND POSSIBLE SEQUENCE

Div. 1		Div. 2	
5	*Banjo and Cello—Imagine That!*	14	*Echo Game—Playbacks!*
13	*Coded Message*	15	*Question and Answer*
4	*Rockin' Sunrise*	8	*Discovering Triads*
5	*Interval Safari*	8	*Broken and Blocked Triads*
26—Solos 2	*Let's Waltz*	9	*Triadic Triumph*
14	*Pitch Detective*	24—Solos 2	*Fanfare*
28—Solos 2	*Little Song*	10	*The Parade*
14	*Echo Game—Clapbacks!*	12	*Triple Treat*
6	*Dotted Quarter Discovery*	16	*The Hound Dawg Song*
7	*Exotic Birds*	12	*Rainbow Leaps*

TEACHER'S NOTES AND TIPS

Musicianship

Major Triads
In Unit 7, students learn that the Tonic (Root), 3rd and 5th (Dominant) of the 5-finger pattern form a major triad. Learning to identify and name triads in both blocked and broken form is an important step in pattern recognition.

Flashcards (F25): Besides naming the Major triad, ask the student to name the Root, the 3rd, or the 5th.

T I P P S

Note that the Practice Plans no longer include **TIPPS** as a reminder for students. Teachers may still need to remind students to follow these basic steps whenever they practice.

Rhythm

The dotted-quarter and the dotted quarter-eighth rhythm can be confusing to students. The progression from eighth notes, to an eighth note tied to a quarter note, to the dotted-quarter eighth rhythm shown in the concept box on p. 6 will help the student understand this rhythm. Teachers must ensure that students count all the eighth notes in the dotted-eighth rhythm: "Ta – i ti ta ta" (pronounced "Ta– ee ti ta ta") or, if counting numerically, 1 & 2 &, etc. continuing to subdivide the beat.

Technique

Rainbow Leaps (p. 12) prepares the student to play an octave. Help students practice the octave leap with a rounded, relaxed hand position. Students with small hands should play with a detached touch but still practice the arched or "rainbow" shaped hand gesture.

Creativity

Students have been playing *Questions and Answers* since Level 1B. In this unit, they learn the difference between a parallel Answer, which begins the same as the Question, and a contrasting Answer, which begins differently. Students should create several parallel and contrasting Answers to each Question before writing their favorite Answer.

LEVEL 2—UNIT 8: PLANNING FOR PREPARATION, PRESENTATION, AND FOLLOW-UP

Preparation
- *Ritardando*
- *a tempo*

Presentation
- Octave
- Fermata
- Key signatures: flat keys
- Solfège

Follow-up
- 5th–6th–5th
- Tonic, Dominant
- Key signatures: sharp keys
- *Crescendo, diminuendo*
- Major triads
- Eighth notes, dotted quarter-eighth
- Upbeat

UNIT 8: OVERVIEW

PAGE	ACTIVITY	PRESENTATION	PREPARATION ▲	SPECIAL ACTIVITY	DIV.
	Repertoire				
20	*Alouette*	Octave; fermata			1
22	*Journey of the Triads*	Octave; fermata		YBTJ!	1
24	*Donkey Riding*	Key signatures: flat keys			2
26	*Leaky Faucet*	Key signatures: flat keys; octave	*Ritardando*	Transpose; Create	2
28	*Jumping Jacks*	Key signatures: flat keys			2
	Solos				
28	*Polka*				1
29	*Turn About*	Key signatures: flat keys			2
30	*Balloons*	Fermata			1
	Finger Gyms				
18	*5-finger Warm-ups*			Transpose	1, 2
21	*Octave Challenge*	Octave		Transpose	1
	Musicianship				
19	*Discovering Octaves*	Octave		F27	1
23	*Discovering Flat Key Signatures*	Key signatures: flat keys		F28	2
29	*Tracing Flats*	Key signatures: flat keys			2
29	*Key Signature Challenge*	Key signatures: flat keys			2
	Rhythm				
30	*Polka Dotted Quarters*				2
30	*Rechargeable Batteries*		*Rit.; a tempo*		1
	Ear Skills				
18	*Interval Safari*	Solfège			1
19	*Interval Safari: Donkey Song*	Octave			1
31	*Mystery Melody*	Key signatures: flat keys			2
31	*Echo Game—Clapbacks!*				2
31	*Echo Game—Playbacks!*				1
	Creativity				
22	*Journey of the Triads*				1
30	*Charged-up Melody*				1

LEVEL 2—UNIT 8: INTEGRATED MUSICIANSHIP AND POSSIBLE SEQUENCE

Div. 1		Div. 2	
31	*Echo Game—Playbacks!*	18	*5-finger Warm-ups* (no. 2)
18	*5-finger Warm-ups* (no. 1)	29—Solos 2	*Turn About*
18	*Interval Safari*	23	*Discovering Flat Key Signatures*
28—Solos 2	*Polka*	24	*Donkey Riding*
19	*Discovering Octaves*	31	*Echo Game—Clapbacks!*
19	*Interval Safari: Donkey Song*	30	*Polka Dotted Quarters*
21	*Octave Challenge*	26	*Leaky Faucet*
20	*Alouette*	27	*Leaky Faucet* (creative)
30—Solos 2	*Balloons*	28	*Jumping Jacks*
22	*Journey of the Triads*	29	*Tracing Flats*
30	*Rechargeable Batteries*	29	*Key Signature Challenge*
30	*Charged-up Melody*	3	*Mystery Melody*

TEACHER'S NOTES AND TIPS

Musicianship
Flat Keys

In Unit 8, key signatures for flat keys are introduced and reinforced in the repertoire. Only the notated key signature is new: students have been playing in Major 5-finger patterns since Unit 2 of Level 2.

Technique

5-finger Warm-ups on p. 18 reviews the 5-finger pattern as well as the 5th–6th–5th accompaniment. It is helpful to remind the student that in these exercises the top note of the 5th moves up a whole step to form a 6th while the bottom note moves down a half step to form the 6th.

Ear Skills
Solfège

In this unit, *Interval Safari* is expanded to include singing the 5-finger pattern using either solfège or the tone numbers of the scale. Some music teachers prefer solfège syllables, which produce a better tone while singing. Other teachers may choose to sing using tone numbers to clearly define each degree of the scale. We leave this choice to the teacher. This type of singing and ear training will be developed throughout Levels 2B, 3, and 4 as students begin to sight-sing melodies before they play. One of the hallmarks of good sight reading is the ability to look at a piece of music and hear what it sounds like (rhythm, melody, harmony, etc.) *before* playing. Even if students cannot sing the melodies in tune, they can hear their piece with relative accuracy before they play. This useful skill is often neglected during piano study.

Interval Safari

Donkey Song—The interval of an octave will stretch the student's ability to sing on pitch. Although it may take several weeks before students are able to sing the song accurately, the *Donkey Song* is a student favorite and is eventually sung with success. Encourage students to sing the octave as if coming from above, i.e., have them tilt the chin down and feel the octave at the top of the throat rather than tilting the chin back and stretching up to the octave, which results in tension and flat pitch.

With the ear skills activity, *Mystery Melody,* which has missing notes, students get to test their inner hearing by completing this familiar folk song. Encourage the student to sing the melody and figure out the title *before* they play the melody.

LEVEL 2—UNIT 9: PLANNING FOR PREPARATION, PRESENTATION, AND FOLLOW-UP

Preparation
- Staccato vs. legato
- Finger crossing
- 7ths
- Eighth-note upbeat

Presentation
- Ostinato
- *Ritardando*
- Tempo and *a tempo*
- Staccato vs. legato

Follow-up
- Octave
- Key signatures
- *Diminuendo*
- Major triads
- Eighth notes, eighth rest, dotted quarter-eighth note
- Pattern Detective
- Solfège

UNIT 9: OVERVIEW

PAGE	ACTIVITY	PRESENTATION	PREPARATION ▲	SPECIAL ACTIVITY	DIV.
	Repertoire				
33	*Russian Dance*	Ostinato; staccato vs. legato			1
34	*Once a Canadian Lad*	*A tempo; ritardando*		Transpose; YBTJ!	2
36	*Hesitation Hop*	Ostinato		Transpose	1
37	*Last Train to Bluesville*	*Ritardando*; ostinato			2
	Solos				
33	*Duet*	*Ritardando*			2
	Finger Gyms				
32	*Balancing Act*		Staccato vs. legato	Transpose	1
38	*Crosswalk*		Finger crossing		2
	Musicianship				
38	*Mix 'n' Match Triads*				2
39	*Leaping Letters*		7ths		1
39	*Keys to Success*				2
	Rhythm				
40	*Tapping Together*				2
	Ear Skills				
32	*Interval Safari*				1
40	*Pattern Detective*				1
41	*Echo Game—Clapbacks!*		Eighth-note upbeat		2
41	*Echo Game—Playbacks!*				1
	Creativity				
41	*Question and Answer*				1
41	*Next Stop Bluesville*	Ostinato			2

LEVEL 2—UNIT 9: INTEGRATED MUSICIANSHIP AND POSSIBLE SEQUENCE

Div. 1		Div. 2	
40	*Pattern Detective*	41	*Echo Game—Clapbacks!*
39	*Leaping Letters*	40	*Tapping Together*
32	*Interval Safari*	34	*Once a Canadian Lad*
32	*Balancing Act*	38	*Mix 'n' Match Triads*
33	*Russian Dance*	37	*Last Train to Bluesville*
36	*Hesitation Hop*	41	*Next Stop Bluesville*
41	*Question and Answer*	32—Solos 2	*Duet*
41	*Echo Game—Playbacks!*	39	*Keys to Success*
		38	*Crosswalk*

TEACHER'S NOTES AND TIPS

Musicianship

Unit 9 introduces Tempo, *a tempo, ritardando,* and a LH ostinato pattern.

Last Train to Bluesville (p. 37) is one of many pieces that allow your student to play the blues. This ostinato is a standard LH jazz accompaniment that prepares the student for more complicated jazz and blues styles.

Leaping Letters (p. 39) prepares the student for the interval of a 7th. In order for the student to learn to sing the 7th, we ask them to sing the octave first and then descend to the 7th. This exercise asks the student to write this pattern before they have to sing it in Unit 10.

Technique

Finger Gym Balancing Act (p. 32) continues to prepare the student to play staccato in the LH against the RH legato phrases. *Russian Dance* (p. 33) is the first repertoire piece to use this technique in an ostinato accompaniment pattern. Have your student practice HS first, paying particular attention to playing the LH staccato notes lightly.

Crosswalk (p. 38): This is the student's first experience with finger crossing in a piece. Remind the student to maintain a rounded hand position and avoid twisting the wrist or raising the elbow.

Ear Skills

Ear skills continue to reinforce the student's ability to discriminate rhythms, intervals and patterns. *Pattern Detective* (p. 40) focuses on rhythm patterns and the ability to discriminate between 5ths and octaves, which can be confusing for students.

LEVEL 2—UNIT 10: PLANNING FOR PREPARATION, PRESENTATION, AND FOLLOW-UP

Preparation
- Finger crossing
- Eighth-note upbeat

Presentation
- Interval: 7th
- Form: AB, ABA
- *D.C. al Fine*

Follow-up
- Octave
- *Crescendo, diminuendo*
- Major triads
- *Ritardando*
- Eighth notes, dotted quarter-eighth
- Fermata
- Variation
- Solfège

UNIT 10: OVERVIEW

PAGE	ACTIVITY	PRESENTATION	PREPARATION ▲	SPECIAL ACTIVITY	DIV.
	Repertoire				
45	*Graceful Swan*	7ths		YBTJ!	1
47	*Yodeler's Holiday*	D.C. al Fine; Form: ABA; 7ths			1
48	*Mexican Dance*	Form: AB		Transpose	2
50	*Polly Wolly Doodle*	Form: AB		Transpose	2
	Solos				
34	*Busybody*	7ths			1
35	*Allegro in C*	ABA; D.C. al Fine			2
36	*Seaside Lullaby*	AB			2
	Finger Gyms				
42	*Tumbling Triads*			Transpose	2
44	*Rainbow 7ths*	7ths			1
52	*Crisscross Fingers*		Finger crossing		2
	Musicianship				
43	*Discovering 7ths*	7ths		F29	1
46	*Fun Form Friends*	Form: AB, ABA			1
52	*Interval Mix-up*				1
53	*Terrific Triads*				2
	Rhythm				
53	*Rhythm Math Game*				1
	Ear Skills				
42	*Interval Safari*				1
43	*Interval Safari: Giraffe Song*	7ths			1
54	*Writing the Rhythm*				2
54	*Echo Game—Clapbacks!*		Eighth-note upbeat		1
54	*Echo Game—Playbacks!*				2
	Creativity				
51	*Doodling Polly*				2
54	*Yodeler's Solo*	D.C. al Fine; ABA; 7ths			1

LEVEL 2—UNIT 10: INTEGRATED MUSICIANSHIP AND POSSIBLE SEQUENCE

Div. 1			Div. 2		
42		*Interval Safari*	35—Solos 2		*Allegro, op. 1, no. 4*
43		*Discovering 7ths*	54		*Echo Game—Playbacks!*
43		*Interval Safari: Giraffe Song*	42		*Tumbling Triads*
44		*Rainbow 7ths*	53		*Terrific Triads*
45		*Graceful Swan*	48		*Mexican Dance*
52		*Interval Mix-up*	50		*Polly Wolly Doodle*
34—Solos 2		*Busybody*	51		*Doodling Polly*
54		*Echo Game—Clapbacks!*	54		*Writing the Rhythm*
53		*Rhythm Math Game*	36—Solos 2		*Seaside Lullaby*
46		*Fun Form Friends*	52		*Crisscross Fingers*
47		*Yodeler's Holiday*			
54		*Yodeler's Solo*			

TEACHER'S NOTES AND TIPS

Musicianship
Form
Throughout Levels 1 and 2, we have asked students to recognize patterns and groups of notes that are the same or different. This concept is expanded to introduce form. Students are asked to discriminate between AB and ABA form as they look for familiar patterns. *D.C. al Fine* is one device that is used to create an ABA form. You may notice that many of the pieces are longer as we introduce more aspects of form.

Movement
To illustrate the form of *Yodeler's Holiday* on p. 47, encourage your student to create a simple dance step for the A section and a contrasting dance pattern for the B section.

Technique
Graceful Swan (p. 45) is a lovely, lyrical piece that students love. The RH 7ths should be played legato if possible. Students with small hands may need to detach the notes lightly to avoid excess stretching and a poor hand position. Many students are able to play a relaxed legato 7th with the help of some teacher modeling. Have the student remember the rainbow exercises: think of playing a very gentle 7th, releasing the thumb as soon as the fifth finger reaches the upper note.

The Finger Gym *Tumbling Triads* (p. 42) serves many purposes. It reinforces blocked and broken triads, Tonic and Dominant, and staccato and legato. Measures 7 and 8 prepare the student for simple contrapuntal playing.

Rhythm
Writing the Rhythm (p. 54) has expanded to two measures. Teachers should continue to use a variety of rhythms including eighth notes and rests, and dotted quarter eighth rhythms.

Ear Skills
Interval Safari
The interval of a 7th is sung more easily by first relating it to the octave. In the *Giraffe Song*, the student sings the octave, and then moves down a 2nd to the seventh before trying to sing the 7th directly.

Tip:
Polly Wolly Doodle (p. 50) is a student favorite. It is a familiar folk song in AB form that uses the 5th–6th–5th accompaniment pattern. Played up to tempo the repeated notes can be tricky. Remind the student to play them with a loose wrist and a relaxed arm. Teachers may also take this opportunity to discuss the balance between melody and accompaniment. The LH melody in mm. 8–12 provides an excellent opportunity for listening to the balance as the melody changes hands.

LEVEL 2—UNIT 11: PLANNING FOR PREPARATION, PRESENTATION, AND FOLLOW-UP

Preparation
- I and V^7
- $\frac{6}{8}$

Presentation
- Finger crossing
- Form: Introduction; *Coda*
- Eighth-note upbeat
- 8va

Follow-up
- Form: AB, ABA
- 6th
- Tonic, Dominant
- Accent
- *Ritardando, a tempo*
- Eighth notes and rests; dotted quarter-eighth
- Fermata
- Staccato vs. legato
- Solfège

UNIT 11: OVERVIEW

PAGE	ACTIVITY	PRESENTATION	PREPARATION ▲	SPECIAL ACTIVITY	DIV.
	Repertoire				
56	*Popcorn Man*	Introduction; finger crossing		YBTJ!	1
58	*March of the Bugs*	8va; eighth-note upbeat		Transpose	1
60	*Melodious Exercise*	8va		Transpose	2
62	*Sea Chanty*	*Coda*			2
	Solos				
38	*Woodpecker Dance*	Introduction			2
40	*Minuetto, op. 1, no. 1*				1
	Finger Gyms				
55	*5-finger Warm-up*		I and V^7	Transpose	2
57	*Easy Over*	Eighth-note upbeat; finger crossing		Transpose	1
	Musicianship				
64	*It's a Match*		I and V^7		1
65	*Name that Tune*				2
	Rhythm				
57	*Upbeat Melodies*	Eighth-note upbeat		F30; Create	1
66	*What's Missing?*	Eighth-note upbeat			1
	Ear Skills				
55	*Interval Safari*				1
66	*Mystery melody*				2
67	*Echo Game—Clapbacks!*		$\frac{6}{8}$		1
67	*Echo Game—Playbacks!*				2
	Creativity				
67	*Question and Answer*				2

LEVEL 2—UNIT 11: INTEGRATED MUSICIANSHIP AND POSSIBLE SEQUENCE

Div. 1			Div. 2		
41—Solos 2	*Minuetto, op. 1, no. 1*		55	*5-finger Warm-up*	
55	*Interval Safari*		60	*Melodious Exercise*	
56	*Popcorn Man*		67	*Echo Game—Playbacks!*	
67	*Echo Game—Clapbacks!*		67	*Question and Answer*	
57	*Upbeat Melodies*		66	*Mystery Melody*	
57	*Upbeat Melodies* (creative)		62	*Sea Chanty*	
57	*Easy Over*		38—Solos 2	*Woodpecker Dance*	
58	*March of the Bugs*		65	*Name that Tune*	
66	*What's Missing?*				
64	*It's a Match*				

TEACHER'S NOTES AND TIPS

Musicianship

The new elements in Unit 11 include further elements of form—introduction and *coda*; 8va; and the eighth-note upbeat. The repertoire becomes more challenging with LH independence, playing in keys with more sharps and flats, and more position shifts within pieces. This is a good time to emphasize and review musicianship skills such as key signatures, Tonic and Dominant, triads, intervals, time signatures, and transposition. The student needs a solid foundation in these elements before proceeding to Level 3, which introduces I and V^7 chords, harmonization, and minor keys.

Finger Gym

Students have played several Finger Gyms in previous units to prepare for playing finger crossovers. *Popcorn Man* (p. 56) uses RH finger 2 crossovers. Encourage the student to keep a relaxed and rounded hand position. The Practice Plan helps the student discover these crossovers before they play.

Tips:

Diabelli's *Melodius Exercise* (p. 60) includes the A section only. It is presented in its original form with Diabelli's duet accompaniment. While this piece is basically a simple melody in C Major, it presents a rhythmic and technical challenge as the student plays the variation sections with eighth rests and off-beat rhythms. It is fun to have the student sight read mm. 1–8 in the lesson, playing with beautiful legato phrasing. The teacher can model by rote an off-beat variation for the student to copy by ear. The student can then discover the secret variations in mm. 8–16 and 25–32. Subdividing the counting (1 & 2 &, etc.) during mm. 1–8 and throughout will help ensure a steady beat with fewer stumbles.

In *Sea Chanty* (p. 62), the *coda* is introduced as another aspect of form. Remember that the *coda* appears after the piece has essentially ended. As an enrichment activity, you might ask the student to play *Sea Chanty*, ending on beat two of m. 16 and ask if the song sounds complete. Then, ask the student to play the song as written and describe the difference—how does the *coda* change the piece?

LEVEL 2—UNIT 12: PLANNING FOR PREPARATION, PRESENTATION, AND FOLLOW-UP

Preparation
- I and V^7
- $\frac{6}{8}$

Presentation
- Common time
- *mf, mp*

Follow-up
- Form: AB, ABA; *D.C. al Fine*
- Introduction
- 8va
- Eighth-note upbeat
- 6th
- 5th–6th–5th
- Major triads
- Finger crossing
- Tonic, Dominant
- *Crescendo, diminuendo*
- Eighth notes; dotted quarter-eighth
- Pitch dictation
- Variation

UNIT 12: OVERVIEW

PAGE	ACTIVITY	PRESENTATION	PREPARATION ▲	SPECIAL ACTIVITY	DIV.
	Repertoire				
70	*Skip to My Lou*	Common time		Transpose	1
72	*Desert Caravan*	*mf; mp*		YBTJ!	1
74	*Riding the Waves*	*mf*; Common time		Transpose	2
79	*Rhythm Ace*	Common time			2
	Solos				
42	*Mountains in Winter*	*mf, mp*; Common time			1
44	*Rhythm Ace*	*mf, mp*			2
	Finger Gyms				
68	*5-finger Climb*		I and V^7	Transpose	1
76	*Over the Top*			Transpose	2
	Musicianship				
69	*Hidden Triads*				1
77	*Musical Crossword*				2
	Rhythm				
76	*Time Signature Workout*	Common time			1
	Ear Skills				
68	*Interval Safari*				2
78	*Pitch Detective*	Common time			2
78	*Echo Game—Clapbacks!*		$\frac{6}{8}$		1
78	*Echo Game—Playbacks!*				2
	Creativity				
71	*Skip to My Lou Variation*	Common time			1
78	*Question and Answer*				2

LEVEL 2—UNIT 12: INTEGRATED MUSICIANSHIP AND POSSIBLE SEQUENCE

Div. 1			Div. 2		
68	*5-finger Climb*		68	*Interval Safari*	
69	*Hidden Triads*		78	*Pitch Detective*	
70	*Skip to My Lou*		76	*Over the Top*	
71	*Skip to My Lou Variation*		78	*Echo Game—Playbacks!*	
76	*Time Signature Workout*		74	*Riding the Waves*	
78	*Echo Game—Clapbacks!*		77	*Musical Crossword*	
72	*Desert Caravan*		79	*Rhythm Ace*	
42—Solos 2	*Mountains in Winter*		78	*Question and Answer*	
			44—Solos 2	*Bouncing on My Bed*	

TEACHER'S NOTES AND TIPS

Musicianship

In Unit 12, we continue the presentation of dynamics with *mf* and *mp*. Building on earlier elements, Common time is introduced as an alternative for $\frac{4}{4}$. As in Unit 11, this is a good time to emphasize and review musicianship skills before moving into Level 3.

Unit 12 reviews many concepts. *5-finger Climb* on p. 68 reviews Tonic and Dominant, 5th–6th–5th (as preparation for I and V^7), and 5-finger patterns. *Hidden Triads* on p. 69 reviews triads. A table of dynamics is presented on p. 73, and musical terms are reviewed in the *Musical Crossword* on p. 77. The student is also given an opportunity to demonstrate their skills at creating Questions and Answers—by writing both the Question and the Answer.

Movement

Students can physically reinforce meter, beat, and dynamics by learning the conducting pattern for $\frac{4}{4}$ meter:

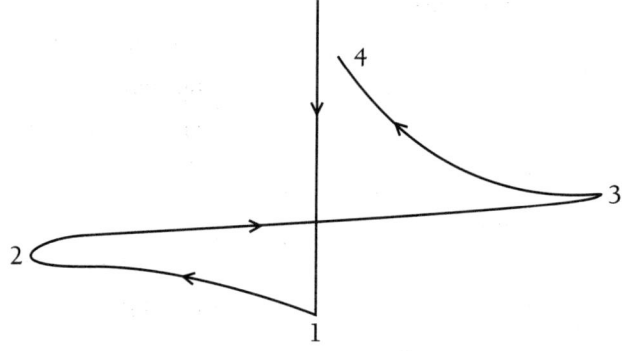

While listening to the CD or MIDI accompaniment, have the student conduct *Riding the Waves* on p. 74, using large motions for the measures that are *f*, smaller four-beat patterns for the measures that are *mf*, and smaller still for the measures marked *p*. *Rhythm Ace* on p. 79 could easily be conducted using the same idea.

Level 3

SCOPE AND SEQUENCE

Unit	Musicianship/Reading	Rhythm	Technique	Ear Skills	Creativity
1	• Review Major 5-finger patterns and triads • I and V^7 chords • 1st and 2nd endings		• Review Major 5-finger patterns and triads • Three-note slur • Damper pedal • I, V^7 chords	• Review intervals: 2nd through octave • Interval Safari, solfège • Melodic dictation	• Review Question and Answer: parallel and contrasting • Variation
2	• Sequence • Harmonizing with I and V^7	• $\frac{6}{8}$, $\frac{9}{8}$ • Dotted quarter rest	• Parallel motion with non-coordinated fingers	• Interval Safari, solfège • Chord progression identification (I and V^7)	• Question and Answer • Variation
3	• Perfect 4th, 5th, octave • Minor 5-finger patterns and triads • Intervals: M3, m3 • Harmonizing with i and V^7 • Minor key signatures: parallel and relative keys		• Minor 5-finger patterns and triads • Minor i and V^7	• Interval Safari, solfège • Intervals: M3, m3 • Melodic dictation • Major vs. minor	• Composition • Question and Answer
4	• Intervals: M2, m2		• Two-note slur	• Interval Safari, solfège • Intervals: M2, m2 • Chord progression identification (i and V^7) • Major vs. minor	• Question and Answer • Composition using ABA
5	• Imitation • IV chord • I–IV–I–V^7–I chord progression		• Legato pedal • I–IV–I–V^7–I chord progression	• Interval Safari, solfège • Melodic dictation • Major vs. minor	• Variation: parallel minor and rhythms
6	• Intervals: M6, m6 • Harmonizing with I, IV, and V^7	• Triplet		• Interval Safari, solfège • Intervals: M6, m6 • Chord progression identification (I, IV, and V^7) • Major vs. minor	• Variation

LEVEL 3—UNIT 1: PLANNING FOR PREPARATION, PRESENTATION, AND FOLLOW-UP

Preparation
- $\frac{6}{8}$
- Sequence
- Minor
- I–V^7–I and harmonizing

Presentation
- Three-note slur
- Damper pedal
- I and V^7 chords
- 1st and 2nd ending

Follow-up
- Intervals: 2nd–octave
- Form: ABA; *D.C. al Fine*; *Coda*
- Key signatures
- *mf, mp*
- *Cres., dim.*
- Staccato vs. legato
- Major triads
- Finger crossing
- 8va
- Common time

UNIT 1: OVERVIEW

PAGE	ACTIVITY	PRESENTATION	PREPARATION ▲	SPECIAL ACTIVITY
	Repertoire			
5	*Trolley Ride*			
8	*Vivace, op. 117, no. 8*	Three-note slur		
10	*Mixed-up Waltz*	Damper pedal; three-note slur		Transpose
14	*Go Tell Aunt Rhody*	I and V^7 chords		Transpose
16	*Singin' the Blues*	1st and 2nd ending; I and V^7; damper pedal		YBTJ!
	Solos			
3	*Out of Breath*			
4	*A Carefree Fellow*	Three-note slur		
4	*Dialogue No. 1*	Three-note slur		
	Finger Gyms			
7	*Drop–Roll–Lift*	Three-note slur	I–V^7–I	Transpose
9	*Press Release*	Damper pedal		
18	*Crossover Caper*	Three-note slur		Transpose
	Musicianship			
6	*Dynamic Discs*			
12	*Tonic (I) and Dominant (V^7)*	I and V^7		Transpose
12	*Building a V^7 Chord*	I and V^7		
12	*Chord Progression*	I and V^7	Harmonizing with I and V^7	
13	*Forming Fives*	I and V^7		
18	*Stair Steps*	Three-note slur	Sequence	
	Rhythm			
19	*Inspector Rhythm*			
	Ear Skills			
6	*Interval Safari*			
20	*Hear, Here!—Melody*			
20	*Clapbacks*		$\frac{6}{8}$	
20	*Playbacks*			
	Creativity			
21	*Question and Answer Phrases*			
21	*Variation on Go Tell Aunt Rhody*		Minor	

TEACHER'S NOTES AND TIPS

Musicianship

I and V⁷ Chords

Tonic chords and Dominant 7th chords are presented along with the I and V^7 symbols and patterns. These chords are related to 5-finger patterns: students are asked to build I and V^7 chords without reference to chord inversions or harmonic function. In elementary music, the student usually encounters the V^7 chord in root position or in 1st inversion with the fifth of the chord omitted. The student should use the formula on p. 12 of *Lesson and Musicianship 3* for building V^7 chords. Practice the I–V^7–I chord progression in several different keys.

Technique

Three-note slur

The three-note slur is introduced in this unit. Teachers should model a beautiful three-note slur with a "down" or drop motion on the first note, a legato roll on the second note, and a light "up" or lifting motion on the third note. Asking the student to say "drop, roll, lift" as they play will remind them of the correct gesture.

Damper pedal

The damper pedal and its symbol are introduced on p. 9. This is the introduction of direct or straight pedaling, in which the student is shown exactly where to put the pedal down and when to release it. Legato, or syncopated pedaling is introduced in Unit 5.

Ear Skills

In *Hear, Here!—Melody* (p. 20), students are asked to discriminate and notate both pitch and rhythm. Teachers will need to play the example several times to allow the student to succeed. (The teacher's example is on the inside back cover of the *Lesson and Musicianship* book.) For example:

• first time—the student listens to the rhythm and then claps it back

• second time—the student notates the rhythm on the blank measures above the staff

• third and fourth time—the student writes the pitches

Creativity

In *Variation on Go Tell Aunt Rhody* (p. 21), students are asked to create a variation by "changing one or more notes in each phrase." Students may change pitch, rhythm, or both. For example, in m. 1, the first half note might be changed to a quarter note followed by two eighths. That same half note could be changed to a quarter note B followed by a quarter note A. The possibilities are endless.

Tip:

Vivace, op. 117, no. 8 (p. 8): The articulation and dynamic markings are Gurlitt's. Here are a couple of options for playing the quarter notes:

1) Play all unmarked quarter notes slightly detached (not staccato).

2) Play all the D and G quarter-note patterns as two-note slurs (e.g., mm. 2, 4, 9–12).

LEVEL 3—UNIT 2: PLANNING FOR PREPARATION, PRESENTATION, AND FOLLOW-UP

Preparation
- Two-note slur
- Minor 3rd

Presentation
- $\frac{6}{8}, \frac{9}{8}$
- Dotted quarter rest
- Sequence
- Harmonizing with I and V^7 chords

Follow-up
- Form: AB, ABA, *D.C. al Fine*
- 1st and 2nd ending
- *mf*
- Three-note slur
- Damper pedal
- Major triads
- I–V^7

UNIT 2: OVERVIEW

PAGE	ACTIVITY	PRESENTATION	PREPARATION ▲	SPECIAL ACTIVITY
	Repertoire			
23	*Study in G*			YBTJ!
26	*Jiggety-Jog*	$\frac{6}{8}$; sequence; harmonizing with I and V^7		Transpose
28	*Tiny Little Whistle Tune*	$\frac{9}{8}$; dotted-quarter rest; sequence		
30	*On the Trampoline*	$\frac{6}{8}$; dotted-quarter rest; harmonizing with I and V^7		
	Solos			
5	*Smooth Sailing*	Harmonizing with I and V^7		
6	*My Favorite Day*			
8	*Melody*			
	Finger Gyms			
22	*Crazy Fingers*			Transpose
31	*Drop–Lift Patterns*	Sequence	Two-note slur	Transpose
	Musicianship			
24	$\frac{6}{8}$ *and* $\frac{9}{8}$ *Time Signatures*	$\frac{6}{8}, \frac{9}{8}$; dotted-quarter rest		F31
24	*Discovering* $\frac{6}{8}$ *and* $\frac{9}{8}$	$\frac{6}{8}, \frac{9}{8}$; dotted-quarter rest		
31	*Sequence Search*	$\frac{6}{8}$		
32	*In Harmony*	Harmonizing with I and V^7; $\frac{6}{8}$		Transpose
	Rhythm			
25	*Countdown*	$\frac{6}{8}, \frac{9}{8}$		
33	*Help! Lost Dogs!*	$\frac{6}{8}, \frac{9}{8}$		
34	*Clapbacks*	$\frac{9}{8}$		
34	*Playbacks*	$\frac{6}{8}$		
	Ear Skills			
22	*Interval Safari Review*			
34	*Chord Progression Hunt*			
	Creativity			
35	*Major Dance*	Harmonizing with I and V^7; $\frac{6}{8}$		
35	*Variation on Jiggety-Jog*	Harmonizing with I and V^7	Minor 3rd	

TEACHER'S NOTES AND TIPS

Musicianship

Sequences

Sequences, which are often used as a compositional tool, are presented on p. 26. We encourage teachers to have students look for patterns and sequences in their pieces as a matter of routine. Identifying elements of form such as patterns, sequences, phrasing, and A and B sections facilitates sight reading and learning new music.

Harmonizing with I and V⁷

Harmonizing with I and V^7 is presented on p. 32. This exercise allows students to harmonize familiar folk songs and melodies by ear. They will also develop a better understanding of their new pieces.

Rhythm

With the introduction of the time signatures $\frac{6}{8}$ and $\frac{9}{8}$, students are encouraged to continue a dual approach to counting. When using syllabic counting, students are able to feel the beat; numeric counting reinforces the placement of the beat within each measure.

We chose "do-bi-di" for counting in $\frac{6}{8}$ and $\frac{9}{8}$ to avoid using ta for both quarter notes and dotted quarter notes. We wanted a syllabic system that would ensure accurate rhythm, and be musical and fun at the same time. Some students like to pretend that they are "scat" singing!

Technique

Crazy Fingers (p. 22) is a Finger Gym that reinforces phrasing and the three-note slur. It also helps develop hand independence as the student plays in parallel motion with non-coordinated fingers.

Drop–Lift Patterns (p. 31) helps develop finger independence and prepares the student for the two-note slur. The *diminuendo* hairpins are used to indicate the drop–lift motion of leaning into the first note of the slur and lifting on the second. Teachers should work toward the down–up, drop–lift, heavy–light motion rather than a drastic difference between loud and soft.

Ear Skills

Chord Progression Hunt (p. 34) is an ear-training activity in which the student learns to discriminate between the I and V^7 chords. This takes only a few seconds in each lesson. Have the student play the patterns to reinforce the chords and sight-reading patterns.

Tips:

Study in G (p. 23): You may wish to add dynamics to this piece (e.g., play mm. 5–8 ***mp***).

Major Dance (p. 35) is a Question and Answer activity that asks the student to compose a phrase and harmonize it. Encourage your students to harmonize simple folk songs, such as *Mary Had a Little Lamb* or *London Bridge*, while playing by ear.

LEVEL 3—UNIT 3: PLANNING FOR PREPARATION, PRESENTATION, AND FOLLOW-UP

Preparation
- Two-note slur

Presentation
- Perfect intervals
- Minor 5-finger patterns and triads
- i–V^7–i
- Minor key signatures
- Intervals: Major and minor 3rds
- Parallel and relative keys

Follow-up
- Common time
- $\frac{6}{8}$, $\frac{9}{8}$
- ABA, *D.C. al Fine*, Introduction, 2nd ending
- Dotted quarter rest
- Sequence
- Three-note slur
- Damper pedal
- I–V^7

UNIT 3: OVERVIEW

PAGE	ACTIVITY	PRESENTATION	PREPARATION ▲	SPECIAL ACTIVITY
	Repertoire			
37	*Etude in C Major*			
40	*Erie Canal*	Minor key signature; i–V^7		
42	*Tarantella*	Minor key signature; i–V^7		Transpose
44	*Perpetual Motion*			YBTJ!
	Solos			
9	*Song,* op. 39, no. 8	Minor key signature		
10	*Beautiful Daisy*	Minor key signature		
12	*Spanish Dance*	Minor key signature		
	Finger Gyms			
36	*Dual Motion*		Two-note slur	Transpose
38	*Parallel Express*	Minor 5-finger patterns and triads; i–V^7; parallel minor		Transpose F32
	Musicianship			
39	*Family Tree—Find Your Relatives!*	Minor key signatures; relative minor		F23
46	*Pat-a-pan*	Minor key signatures; harmonizing with i and V^7		
48	*Tempo Terms*	Musical tempos		
49	*Major/minor League – Interval Baseball*	Major and minor 3rds		
	Rhythm			
48	*Down for the Count*			
	Ear Skills			
36	*Interval Safari Review*	Perfect Intervals: P4, P5, P8		
47	*Interval Safari: Panda Song*	Minor 3rd		F33
50	*Hear, Here!—Melody*			
50	*Clapbacks*			
50	*Playbacks*	Minor 5-finger pattern		
51	*Major–minor Game*	Major and minor triads		
	Creativity			
51	*Tarantella II*	Harmonizing with i and V^7		

UNIT BY UNIT DISCUSSION

TEACHER'S NOTES AND TIPS

Musicianship

Minor 5-finger Patterns and Triads

Minor 5-finger patterns and triads are introduced on p. 38 and are related to Major 5-finger patterns. Students learn to change from Major to minor by lowering the third note of a 5-finger pattern, or the third of a chord by one half step. When introducing the i–V^7–i progression, point out that the V^7 chord remains the same for both the Major and minor patterns. The i and V^7 chords are used in repertoire and exercises. Encourage students to discover and name or label these chords. Harmonizing with i and V^7 is introduced on p. 46 with *Pat-a-pan*.

Parallel Express (p. 38) introduces the term parallel minor and challenges students to play and transpose to all twelve Major and parallel minor keys. Begin by having students play the Major pattern followed by the minor. Eventually they will be able to play the minor pattern without playing the Major pattern.

The term relative minor is introduced on p. 39. In *Family Tree—Find Your Relatives* (p. 39), students are asked to name the Major key and the relative minor key. This type of activity allows students to gain familiarity with the key families and key signatures before learning Major and minor scales in Level 4.

Ear Skills

In this unit, sight singing using solfège or tone numbers expands to include the octave.

On p. 47, minor 3rds are introduced. Relate the minor intervals to the corresponding Major intervals, both on the staff and aurally. It is very important to sing both the *Cuckoo Bird Song* and the *Panda Song*, and to drill both Major and minor 3rds in the ear-training games for intervals. In *Major–minor Game* (p. 51), students are asked to discriminate between Major and minor intervals.

Tip:

Challenge students to practice until they can play all twelve Major and minor patterns in a row, or the twelve patterns with their eyes closed. These fun challenges produce lasting rewards for both student and teacher.

Etude in C Major (p. 37): We suggest detaching the chords in mm. 3 and 11.

LEVEL 3—UNIT 4: PLANNING FOR PREPARATION, PRESENTATION, AND FOLLOW-UP

Preparation
- Triplet

Presentation
- Two-note slur
- Intervals: Major and minor 2nds

Follow-up
- $\frac{6}{8}$, $\frac{9}{8}$
- Dotted quarter rest
- AB, ABA, 1st and 2nd ending
- Minor 5-finger patterns
- Minor key signatures
- Major and minor 3rds
- Sequence
- Three-note slur
- Harmonizing with i–V^7

UNIT 4: OVERVIEW

PAGE	ACTIVITY	PRESENTATION	PREPARATION ▲	SPECIAL ACTIVITY
	Repertoire			
52	Etude, op. 70, no. 16			
54	Peasant Dance	Two-note slur		Transpose
57	On a Greek Island	Major and minor 2nds		
58	Camel Ride	Major and minor 2nds; two-note slur		YBTJ!
	Solos			
14	Country Dance	Two-note slur		
16	A Little Scherzo, op. 39, no. 6	Two-note slur		
	Finger Gyms			
53	Down–Up Dance	Two-note slur		Transpose
60	Parallel Warm-ups			Transpose
	Musicianship			
56	Intervals, Intervals, Intervals	Major and minor 2nds		F34
56	More Intervals, Intervals, Intervals	Major and minor 2nds		
60	Grandma Grunts			
61	Music, Music, Music			
	Rhythm			
62	Grandma's Cupcakes			
	Ear Skills			
63	Interval Safari: Quiet Little Mouse Song	Minor 2nd		
64	Chord Progression Hunt			
64	Clapbacks		Triplet	
64	Playbacks			
65	Major–minor Game			
	Creativity			
65	Minor Dance			

TEACHER'S NOTES AND TIPS

Technique

Two-note slurs are presented on p. 53 and used in *Down–Up Dance*. Remind the student to maintain a relaxed wrist and a drop–lift or down–up gesture, lifting on the second note.

The two-note slur is combined with the three-note slur in *On a Greek Island* (p. 57). Practicing first slowly with an exaggerated motion and then up to tempo with a light drop–lift motion will encourage accurate and relaxed slurs.

Ear Skills

Minor 2nds are introduced in this unit. Remember to relate each minor interval to the corresponding Major interval. Include both harmonic and melodic minor 2nds in all ear-training activities. Have the student discover Major and minor 2nds in *Camel Ride* (p. 58) and other repertoire.

The student is asked to sing *Grandma Grunts* (p. 60) using solfège or tone numbers. This is the first time students have been asked to apply this skill to a song. The goal is for students to be able to see what they hear and hear what they see. Eventually students will be able to look at a melody and use their inner hearing to know how it will sound. They should be able to look at any melody, sing it aloud, or hum it to themselves using solfège or numbers.

Students are also asked to harmonize *Grandma Grunts*. Encourage them to sing and play it in other keys. Their ability to sing, play, harmonize, and transpose these simple songs is a step toward comprehensive musicianship.

Creativity

Minor Dance (p. 65) is a Question and Answer activity in a minor key. Students combine their *Minor Dance* with *Major Dance* from Unit 2 to create an ABA composition. This reinforces form and introduces new compositional tools and variation techniques.

Enrichment Repertoire

Celebrate Piano!™ has been designed to prepare the student to play in a variety of musical styles such as those contained in *Celebration Series*®, *The Piano Odyssey*®, published by The Frederick Harris Music Co., Limited.

For additional Level 3, Unit 4 repertoire, play the following pieces from *Celebration Series*®, *The Piano Odyssey*®, Piano Repertoire 1:
- *Minuet in D Major*, T 460 by Jeremiah Clarke
- *Happy Times* by Vladimir Blok

LEVEL 3—UNIT 5: PLANNING FOR PREPARATION, PRESENTATION, AND FOLLOW-UP

Preparation
- Subdominant (IV) chord
- Harmonizing with I, IV, V^7
- Triplet
- Syncopation

Presentation
- Legato pedal
- Subdominant (IV) chord
- I–IV–I–V^7–I chord progression
- Imitation

Follow-up
- $\frac{6}{8}$
- AB, ABA, 1st and 2nd ending
- Two- and three-note slurs
- Minor key signatures
- Major and minor 2nds
- Damper pedal
- Major and minor triads
- Sequence
- Harmonizing with I–V^7 and i–V^7

UNIT 5: OVERVIEW

PAGE	ACTIVITY	PRESENTATION	PREPARATION ▲	SPECIAL ACTIVITY
	Repertoire			
67	*Etude, op. 82, no. 17*	Imitation		
69	*Morning Dew*	Legato pedal		
70	*Evening Sunset*	Legato pedal		YBTJ!
74	*For He's a Jolly Good Fellow*	IV chord		Transpose
76	*Follow the Leader*	IV chord		
	Solos			
17	*Staccato and Legato*	Imitation		
18	*Angelfish*	Legato pedal		
20	*Night Song*	Legato pedal		
	Finger Gyms			
66	*Reach and Slur*		IV chord	Transpose
68	*Pedal Moods*	Legato pedal		
	Musicianship			
72	*Building a IV Chord*	IV chord		
73	*Scoring Four*	IV chord		
73	*Chord Progression Parade*	I–IV–I–V^7–I chord progression	Harmonizing with I, IV, V^7	Transpose
77	*Measuring Intervals*			
77	*Slavic Melody*			Transpose
78	*Relative Investigations*			
	Rhythm			
78	*Rhythm Hut*			
	Ear Skills			
66	*Interval Safari: Major and minor 2nds and 3rds*			
79	*Hear, Here!—Melody*			
79	*Clapbacks*		Triplet; syncopation	
79	*Playbacks*			
80	*Major–minor Game*			
	Creativity			
80	*Changing Grandma's Tune*			

TEACHER'S NOTES AND TIPS

Musicianship

Imitation

The Gurlitt *Etude* on p. 67, which introduces imitation between the hands, is an excellent preparation for contrapuntal playing. Asking the students to label or bracket the imitation will help them see the patterns.

IV Chord

The Subdominant chord is presented on p. 72. Students are asked to build the IV chord in relation to the I chord. (Chord inversions are presented in Level 4.) In repertoire at this level, students will most often encounter the I, IV, and V^7 chords in the positions shown. Encourage your students to play and transpose *Chord Progression Parade* (p. 73) to all keys.

Also, remember to ask students to discover and label I, IV, and V^7 chords in their repertoire.

Technique

Legato Pedal

Legato (syncopated) pedaling is presented on p. 68. Carefully guide your students as they learn to listen for clean pedaling and help them identify where the pedal changes should occur. You may wish to ask students to play white-key triads HS ascending (C, D, E, etc.), changing the pedal on each triad.

Coordinating the foot and hand is essential. Students will need to practice a quick pedal change, making sure the pedal is down while the hand is moving, and changing the pedal with a quick up–down motion as the chord is played. Stress the importance of keeping the heel on the floor, with the ball of the foot on the pedal and maintaining contact with the pedal. Lifting the foot off the pedal will result in a "slapping" sound.

The pedal markings on *Morning Mood* prepare for *Morning Dew*. The pedal markings on *Sunset Mood*, which do not require changing the pedal on every triad, prepare the student for *Evening Sunset*.

Tip:

Etude, op. 82, no. 17 (p. 67): Lifting at the end of an overlapping phrase is a challenge in this piece. Have the student practice slowly, with an exaggerated lift on the "and" of every beat 4.

Enrichment Repertoire

For additional Level 3, Unit 5 repertoire, play the following pieces from *Celebration Series®*, *The Piano Odyssey®*, Piano Repertoire 1:
• *Dialogue (Canon)* by Jon George
• *Dorian Invention* by Pierre Gallant

LEVEL 3—UNIT 6: PLANNING FOR PREPARATION, PRESENTATION, AND FOLLOW-UP

Preparation
- Minor 6th
- Sixteenth notes
- Syncopation

Presentation
- Triplet
- Intervals: Major and minor 6ths
- Harmonizing with I, IV, and V^7

Follow-up
- $\frac{6}{8}$
- 1st and 2nd ending
- Two- and three-note slurs
- Minor 5-finger patterns
- Major and minor 2nds and 3rds
- Damper pedal
- Sequence
- Harmonizing with I and V^7

UNIT 6: OVERVIEW

PAGE	ACTIVITY	PRESENTATION	PREPARATION ▲	SPECIAL ACTIVITY
	Repertoire			
83	*Fanfare Sonatina*	Triplet		
86	*Dancin' Shoes*	Major and minor 6ths; triplet		YBTJ!
88	*A Moonlight Waltz*	Major and minor 6ths		YBTJ!
95	*Sparklers*			
	Solos			
22	*Minuetto*	Triplet		
23	*March of the Terrible Trolls*	Triplet		
	Finger Gyms			
81	*Flat Out*		Minor 6th	Transpose
90	*Major–minor Shuffle*			Transpose
	Musicianship			
84	*Sixth Sense*	Major and minor 6ths		F36
90	*Interval Scramble*	Major and minor 6ths		
91	*I Had a Cow*	Harmonizing with I, IV, and V^7		
	Rhythm			
82	*Discovering Triplets*	Triplet		F35
92	*Rhythm Ripples*	Triplet		
	Ear Skills			
81	*Interval Safari: Major and minor 2nds and 3rds*			
85	*Interval Safari: Lizard Song*	Minor 6th		
93	*Chord Progression Hunt*			
93	*Clapbacks*	Triplet	Sixteenth notes; syncopation	
93	*Playbacks*			
94	*Major–minor Game*			
	Creativity			
94	*Oranges and Lemons*			Transpose

TEACHER'S NOTES AND TIPS

Rhythm

Triplets

Triplets are introduced in Unit 6. Students are encouraged to count with the tri-ple-tee syllables. Reinforce the fact that a triplet equals one beat. The teacher may wish to supplement this with a discussion of meter and/or accents within the measure.

Ear Skills

Minor 6ths are introduced in this unit. Remember to relate the Major 6th to the minor 6th. Continue to sing all of the Interval Safari songs. It is helpful to present the Major 6th as a Perfect 5th plus a whole step and the minor 6th as a Perfect 5th plus a half step. This helps the student build and write the intervals with success.

Tips:

A Moonlight Waltz on p. 88 offers a variety of technical challenges such as shifting hand positions, contrapuntal writing, finger crossovers, and pedaling. Create practice strategies for these challenges. For example, for pedaling, have the student practice pedal alone while counting, or practice the LH while pedaling.

Sparklers (p. 95): The D♯ may be omitted from the four-note chords if the student has difficulty changing from three-note to four-note chords.

Enrichment Repertoire

For additional Level 3, Unit 6 repertoire, play the following pieces from *Celebration Series®, The Piano Odyssey®*, Piano Repertoire 1:
* *The Bear in the Forest*, op. 11, no. 6 by Vladimir Blok
* *On the Bridge at Avignon*, arr. Pierre Gallant

Level 4

SCOPE AND SEQUENCE

Unit	Musicianship/Reading	Rhythm	Technique	Ear Skills	Creativity
1	• Intervals: M7, m7 • Accompaniment styles in $\frac{3}{4}$	• Syncopation	• Accompaniment styles in $\frac{3}{4}$	• Interval Safari, solfège • Intervals: M7, m7 • Major vs. minor • Melodic and rhythmic dictation	• Question and Answer
2	• Tenuto • Whole-tone scale • Accompaniment styles in $\frac{4}{4}$	• Sixteenth notes and rests	• Accompaniment styles in $\frac{4}{4}$	• Interval Safari, solfège • Intervals: M6, m6, M7, m7 • Major vs. minor • Harmonic dictation	• Question and Answer: ABA
3	• Canon • Chord inversions • Dominant 7th chord (V^7) • Major scales in tetrachords		• Chord inversion fingering • Major scales in tetrachords	• Interval Safari, solfège • Intervals: M2, m2, M3, m3, M6, m6, M7, m7 • Melodic and rhythmic dictation	• Composition using the whole-tone scale
4	• Binary form • Accompaniment styles in $\frac{6}{8}$	• Sixteenth-note combinations • Accelerando	• C Major scale: HS, two octaves • C Major scale: contrary motion	• Interval Safari, solfège • Major vs. minor • Chord progression identification	• Question and Answer: harmonized
5	• Pentatonic scale	• Dotted eighth and sixteenth notes	• Scale fingering rule • G and F Major scales: HS, two octaves	• Interval Safari, solfège • Melodic and rhythmic dictation	• Question and Answer: harmonized
6	• Subdominant (iv) chord in minor • i–iv–i–V7–i • Chromatic scale	• Cut time or Alla breve	• Relative minor scales: a minor (harmonic, natural): HS, two octaves • Chromatic scale	• Interval Safari, solfège • Mystery melody • Major vs. minor • Harmonic dictation	• Improvisation: chord inversions

LEVEL 4—UNIT 1: PLANNING FOR PREPARATION, PRESENTATION, AND FOLLOW-UP

Preparation
- Sixteenth notes

Presentation
- Syncopation
- Intervals: Major and minor 7ths
- Accompaniment styles in $\frac{3}{4}$

Follow-up
- Triplet
- $\frac{6}{8}$
- Sequence
- Major and minor 2nds, 3rds, and 6ths
- Harmonizing with I–IV–V^7–I
- Major and minor key signatures
- Two- and three-note slurs
- Legato pedal

UNIT 1: OVERVIEW

PAGE	ACTIVITY	PRESENTATION	PREPARATION ▲	SPECIAL ACTIVITY
	Repertoire			
6	*Celebration*			
10	*Honey, You Can't Love One*	Syncopation		Transpose
12	*Takin' it Easy*	Syncopation		YBTJ!
16	*In Sync*	Minor 7ths; syncopation		
18	*Etude, op. 777, no. 3*	Accompaniment styles in $\frac{3}{4}$		Transpose
	Solos			
24	*Slightly Jazzy*	Syncopation		
26	*Umbrellas*	Major and minor 7ths		
	Finger Gyms			
8	*Look Out Below!*			Transpose
15	*Marching 5ths, 6ths, and 7ths*	Major and minor 7ths		
	Musicianship			
14	*Seventh Inning Stretch*	Major and minor 7ths		F38
17	*Playing in Style*	Accompaniment styles in $\frac{3}{4}$		Transpose
19	*Marching Chords*			Transpose
	Rhythm			
9	*Syncopated Station*	Syncopation		F37
19	*Rhythm Round-up*	Syncopation		
	Ear Skills			
8	*Interval Safari Review*			
15	*Interval Safari: Calico Cat Song*	Minor 7th		
20	*Hear, Here!—Melody*			
20	*Major–minor Game*			
21	*Clapbacks*	Syncopation	Sixteenth notes	
21	*Playbacks*			
	Creativity			
21	*Sunrise Waltz*	Accompaniment styles in $\frac{3}{4}$		

TEACHER'S NOTES AND TIPS

Level 4 of *Celebrate Piano!*™ helps students make a smooth transition into late elementary and early intermediate literature. New elements are introduced such as: syncopation; sixteenth notes and their combinations; accompaniment styles; and Major and minor scales. Hand independence is developed further, leading into contrapuntal playing. Upon completion of this Level, students are well grounded in comprehensive musicianship and are ready to move on to a wide variety of literature from classical to jazz and pop.

This is a good time to review all of the Interval Safari songs, Major and minor 5-finger patterns and triads, the I–IV–I–V^7–I chord progression, and Major and minor key signatures.

Musicianship

Minor 7ths are introduced on p. 14. Remember to relate the minor 7th to the Major 7th and to sing both songs for comparison. Think of the minor 7th as an octave minus a whole step and the Major 7th as an octave minus a half step.

We suggest that you continue to encourage your students to improvise their own melodies and/or play folk melodies such as *Home on the Range* and *Down in the Valley*. Have them harmonize the melody using one of the accompaniment styles presented on p. 17.

Note that chord names (lead sheet symbols) are introduced in *Playing in Style* on p. 17. Students are more likely to encounter these symbols than Roman numerals in current music editions.

Rhythm

Syncopation

Syncopation is introduced on p. 9. Teachers and students should focus on the shifting accent and practice counting and playing a variety of syncopated patterns. Have the student chant the syncopated rhythm while tapping a steady beat with the foot.

Tip:

Etude, op. 777, no. 3 (p. 18): We recommend playing a two-note slur on beats 1 and 2 of the LH. Note that in mm. 3, 7, 10, and 15, each hand plays a different articulation.

Enrichment Repertoire

For additional Level 4, Unit 1 repertoire, play the following pieces from *Celebration Series®, The Piano Odyssey®*, Piano Repertoire 1:
• *Duet for One* by Christopher Norton

LEVEL 4—UNIT 2: PLANNING FOR PREPARATION, PRESENTATION, AND FOLLOW-UP

Preparation
- Scale fingering

Presentation
- Sixteenth notes and rests
- Tenuto
- Whole-tone scale
- Accompaniment styles in $\frac{4}{4}$

Follow-up
- Triplet
- Syncopation
- $\frac{6}{8}$, $\frac{9}{8}$
- Imitation
- M7 and m7
- I–IV–V^7–I
- Major and minor key signatures
- Accompaniment styles in $\frac{3}{4}$
- Two- and three-note slurs
- Legato pedal

UNIT 2: OVERVIEW

PAGE	ACTIVITY	PRESENTATION	PREPARATION ▲	SPECIAL ACTIVITY
	Repertoire			
24	*Arietta in C, op. 42, no. 5*	Sixteenth notes		YBTJ!
27	*Changing Voices*	Tenuto; sixteenth notes		
28	*Time Machine*	Whole-tone scale; sixteenth notes		YBTJ!
30	*A Joke*	Whole-tone scale; tenuto; sixteenth notes		
31	*Melody for Left Hand op. 108, no. 12*			Transpose
	Solos			
27	*Seventh Heaven*			
28	*Folk Song*			
29	*Mysterious Mirrors*	Sixteenth notes; whole-tone scale		
	Finger Gyms			
22	*Triple Cross*		Scale fingering	Transpose
26	*Sixteenth Shuffle*	Tenuto; sixteenth notes		
	Musicianship			
26	*Circle of 5ths*			
32	*Stylin' Susanna*	Accompaniment styles in $\frac{4}{4}$		Transpose
	Rhythm			
23	*Discovering Sixteenths*	Sixteenth notes and rests		F39
33	*Key Rhythms*	Sixteenth notes		
	Ear Skills			
22	*Interval Safari*			
33	*Major–minor Game*			
34	*Hear, Here!—Harmony*			
34	*Clapbacks*			
34	*Playbacks*			
	Creativity			
35	*Sunset Waltz*			
35	*Sunrise–Sunset–Sunrise Waltz*			

TEACHER'S NOTES AND TIPS

Musicianship

Circle of 5ths

Circle of 5ths (p. 26) reviews the Major key signatures and introduces the relationship of keys a fifth apart. Understanding the Circle of 5ths is a valuable tool. You may wish to encourage your student to practice naming or playing the Tonic notes around the Circle of 5ths at the piano and away from the piano.

Whole-tone Scale

In the presentation of the whole-tone scale (p. 28), teachers may wish to challenge their students to start on any note and build a whole-tone scale. This will help students realize that there really are only two possible whole-tone scales (the notes are the same but with a different starting position).

Alberti Bass

Students may need additional practice with the Alberti bass accompaniment pattern (p. 32). Be sure to have your student warm up in the key and practice the Alberti bass with the I, IV, and V^7 chords before playing *Stylin' Susanna*.

Rhythm

Sixteenth notes and rests are presented in Unit 2. Sixteenth notes and their combinations will be presented later in this level. Count carefully, subdividing the beat using syllabic or numeric counting. The student may whisper "rest" or whisper the syllable for the rest.

Finger Gym

Triple Cross (p. 22) helps prepare the student for a variety of finger crossings and scales. Students find it challenging and fun to play this exercise.

Ear Skills

In *Hear, Here!–Harmony* (p. 34), the student is asked to discriminate between I, IV, and V^7 chords. Students have been playing these chords for several units and usually have no problem hearing and writing the correct chord symbol.

Tips:

Time Machine (p. 28): Have the student experiment by playing with the pedal depressed half way. Discuss how this changes the sound.

Melody for Left Hand, op. 108, no. 12 (p. 31): Encourage the student to label all the RH chords. (Chord symbols are provided for mm. 7 and 8 because m. 7 has a 4-3 suspension which resolves in m. 8.) This piece provides an excellent opportunity to work on balance between the hands.

Arietta in C, op. 42 (p. 24): The LH quarter notes may be played detached to contrast the RH, or they may be played legato.

Enrichment Repertoire

For additional Level 4, Unit 2 repertoire, play the following pieces from *Celebration Series®, The Piano Odyssey®*, Piano Repertoire 1:
• *Spooks* by Clifford Poole

LEVEL 4—UNIT 3: PLANNING FOR PREPARATION, PRESENTATION, AND FOLLOW-UP

Preparation
• Sixteenth-note combinations

Presentation
• Canon
• Chord inversions
• Major scales in tetrachords
• Dominant 7th chord

Follow-up
• Triplet
• Sixteenth notes and rests
• Syncopation
• Sequence
• Imitation
• M6, m6, M7, m7
• I–IV–V^7–I
• Whole-tone scale
• Tenuto
• Legato pedal

UNIT 3: OVERVIEW

PAGE	ACTIVITY	PRESENTATION	PREPARATION ▲	SPECIAL ACTIVITY
	Repertoire			
37	*My Shadow*	Canon		Transpose
39	*Gavotte*	Chord inversions		
40	*City Lights*	Chord inversions		YBTJ!
43	*The Harp*	Major scales in tetrachords		Transpose
44	*Jump and Run*	Major scales in tetrachords		
46	*Minuet in G*	Dominant 7th chord		
	Solos			
30	*Tropical Island*			
32	*Dance*, op. 108, no. 1	Dominant 7th chord; chord inversions		
	Finger Gyms			
36	*Follow Me!*			Transpose
38	*Triad Procession*	Chord inversions		Transpose; F40
42	*Chain-link Tetrachords*	Major scales in tetrachords		Transpose
	Musicianship			
45	*Building 7th Chords*	Dominant 7th chord		
47	*Homeward Bound*	Dominant 7th chord		
48	*Inviting Inversions*	Chord inversions		
48	*Inversion Therapy*	Chord inversions		
	Rhythm			
49	*Sound Off*			
	Ear Skills			
36	*Interval Safari*			
49	*Clapbacks*		Sixteenth-note combinations	
49	*Playbacks*			
50	*Hear, Here!—Melody*			
	Creativity			
50	*Outer Limits*			

TEACHER'S NOTES AND TIPS

Musicianship

Chord Inversions

Chord inversions and their fingerings are presented on p. 38. We use the terms Root position, 1st inversion, and 2nd inversion.

Tetrachord Scales

Tetrachord scales, presented on p. 42, provide a building block for presenting the Major scales in a theoretical context. Playing scales first in tetrachord position allows the student to focus on understanding the arrangement of whole steps and half steps in the scale. (Traditional scales and their fingerings are presented in Unit 4.)

Tips:

Triad Procession (p. 38): Have the student practice this activity until the inversion shifts can be done without looking at the hands.

The Harp (p. 43): This is a good piece for experimenting with rubato in mm. 3–4 and 9–10.

Minuet in G (p. 46): We recommend playing the LH detached (not staccato).

Chain-link Tetrachords (p. 42)

Linking the tetrachords of the scale reinforces the Circle of 5ths.

Enrichment Repertoire

For additional Level 4, Unit 3 repertoire, play the following pieces from *Celebration Series®, The Piano Odyssey®*, Piano Repertoire 1:

- *The Hunt*, op. 117, no. 15 by Cornelius Gurlitt (p. 14)
- *March (Lydian Mode)* by David Duke
- *Climb up on an Elephant* by Nancy Telfer

LEVEL 4—UNIT 4: PLANNING FOR PREPARATION, PRESENTATION, AND FOLLOW-UP

Preparation
- Dotted eighth and sixteenth patterns

Presentation
- Binary form
- Sixteenth-note combinations
- Accelerando
- C Major scale fingering
- Accompaniment styles in $\frac{6}{8}$

Follow-up
- Major scales in tetrachords
- Imitation
- M6, m6, M7, m7
- I–IV–V^7–I
- Chord inversions
- Whole-tone scale
- Tenuto
- Legato pedal

UNIT 4: OVERVIEW

PAGE	ACTIVITY	PRESENTATION	PREPARATION ▲	SPECIAL ACTIVITY
	Repertoire			
52	*Minuet in F*	Binary form		
54	*Scherzino*	Accelerando; sixteenth-note combinations		YBTJ!
56	*Classical Criss-Cross*	Sixteenth-note combinations		YBTJ!
59	*Allegro*	C Major scale fingering		
	Solos			
33	*Square Dance*	Sixteenth-note combinations		
34	*Street Performers*	Sixteenth-note combinations		
36	*Bagatelle*	Binary form; accompaniment styles in $\frac{6}{8}$		
	Finger Gyms			
51	*Mixed-up Triads*			Transpose
58	*Scaling in C Major*	C Major scale fingering		
60	*Scaling*	C Major scale fingering		
	Musicianship			
60	*Up to Speed*			
61	*Charlie Over the Water*	Accompaniment styles in $\frac{6}{8}$		Transpose
62	*Circle of 5ths*			
	Rhythm			
53	*Sixteenth-note Combos*	Sixteenth-note combinations		F41
	Ear Skills			
51	*Interval Safari*			
63	*Chord Progression Hunt*			
63	*Clapbacks*	Sixteenth-note combinations	Dotted eighth and sixteenth patterns	
63	*Playbacks*			
64	*Major–minor Game*			
	Creativity			
64	*What's the Answer?*			

TEACHER'S NOTES AND TIPS

Musicanship

Accompaniment styles in $\frac{6}{8}$ are presented on p. 61. In *Charlie over the Water* (p. 61), students apply the comprehensive musicianship skills they have learned. They sight-sing the melody, harmonize with chords, select an accompaniment pattern, and transpose.

Encourage your students to apply these comprehensive musicianship skills to other folk songs, popular songs, and their own improvised melodies.

Technique

The C Major scale and its fingering is presented on p. 58. Encourage the student to maintain a good hand position with a level forearm and wrist. While playing scales, students should avoid twisting the wrist or extending the elbow.

Ear Skills

In this unit, students are asked to transfer solfège to the Interval Safari songs for Major intervals. Have the student sing familiar folk songs using solfège.

Tip:

On p. 62, emphasize the importance of being able to name the keys and key signatures around the Circle of 5ths.

Enrichment Repertoire

For additional Level 4, Unit 4 repertoire, play the following pieces from *Celebration Series*®, *The Piano Odyssey*®, Piano Repertoire 1:

* *Minuet in C Major,* op. 38, no. 4 by Johann Wilhelm Hässler
* *A Happy Tale,* op. 36, no. 31 by Alexander Gedike

LEVEL 4—UNIT 5: PLANNING FOR PREPARATION, PRESENTATION, AND FOLLOW-UP

Preparation
- G Major scale

Presentation
- Pentatonic scale
- Dotted eighth-sixteenth
- G and F Major scales

Follow-up
- Sixteenth-note combinations
- Syncopation
- Canon
- C Major scale
- M6, m6, M7, m7
- I–IV–V^7–I
- Chord inversions
- Accompaniment styles
- Legato pedal

UNIT 5: OVERVIEW

PAGE	ACTIVITY	PRESENTATION	PREPARATION ▲	SPECIAL ACTIVITY
	Repertoire			
66	*The Zheng*	Pentatonic scale		
69	*Good Little Girl*	Dotted eighth–sixteenth		Transpose
71	*Moderato*	G Major scale		
72	*The Music Box*	F Major scale		YBTJ!
	Solos			
37	*Etude,* op. 82, no. 65			
38	*Old Friends*	G Major scale		
	Finger Gyms			
65	*Don't Be Cross!*		G Major scale	Transpose
70	*Scaling in G Major*	G Major scale		
70	*Scaling in F Major*	F Major scale		
	Musicianship			
74	*Scaling Adventures*	G and F Major scales		
75	*Can-Do Canon*			Transpose
75	*Inversion Scramble*			
77	*Little Tommy Tinker*			Transpose
	Rhythm			
68	*Sixteenth-note Discovery*	Dotted eighth–sixteenth		F12
76	*Pinch Hitters*	G Major scale; dotted eighth–sixteenth		
	Ear Skills			
65	*Interval Safari*			
77	*Hear, Here!—Melody*			
78	*Clapbacks*			
78	*Playbacks*			
	Creativity			
78	*You Name It*			

TEACHER'S NOTES AND TIPS

Musicianship

Pentatonic Scales

Pentatonic scales are presented on p. 66. Ask your student to play the two pentatonic scales written on p. 66 before they play *The Zheng* (pronounced Cheng).

Technique

The *Scale Fingering Rule* is presented on p. 70 along with the G Major scale.

Scale Fingering

Teach students that there are groups of scales that have the same fingering. Understanding the fingering rules for each group will enable them to learn and remember the scale fingerings more quickly. A student should not have to rely on a scale book to learn fingering.

General Scale Groups:

Group 1: C, G, D, A, E Major
Group 2: B, F♯, C♯ Major
Group 3: A♭, E♭, B♭, F Major

We present the Group 1 scales plus the F Major scale and fingerings in Level 4. Refer to the scale review chart on pp. 94–95 of the *Lesson and Musicianship* book for other scales.

Students will recognize fragments of scales in their pieces, and realize that by learning scale fingerings, they can more readily play these pieces.

Rhythm

The dotted eighth–sixteenth pattern is presented on p. 68. We encourage students to subdivide the beat as they count and play.

Remind students to tap and count the rhythm patterns for *Good Little Girl* (p. 69) before they play. Have your student tap the RH rhythm alone before

tapping HT. The student might tap the RH as you tap the LH and vice versa. Finally, have the student tap HT paying careful attention to the new dotted eighth–sixteenth pattern.

Creativity

Can-Do Canon (p. 75) provides an excellent opportunity for students to create their own canon. This structured exercise gives them the basis for a secure start. Encourage them to write imitative pieces and canons on their own. This is excellent preparation for Baroque and Classical imitative styles.

Tips:

The Zheng (p. 66): Discuss the transition from m. 1, which is played freely, to m. 2, which requires a steady pulse. Have the student count in while holding the fermata in m. 1.

Good Little Girl (p. 69): Phrasing has been added to clarify the phrase structure.

Moderato (p. 71): Experiment with LH articulation. The quarter notes may be played legato or detached.

Enrichment Repertoire

For additional Level 4, Unit 5 repertoire, play the following pieces from *Celebration Series®, The Piano Odyssey®,* Piano Repertoire 1:

- *The Hunting Horns and the Echo* by Daniel Gottlob Türk
- *German Dance,* Hob. IX:22, no. 3 by Franz Joseph Haydn
- *Minuet in F Major,* K 2 by Wolfgang Amadeus Mozart
- *The Jolly Fiddler,* op. 41, no. 5 by Grigori Frid
- *Teapot Invention* by Andrew Markow

LEVEL 4—UNIT 6: PLANNING FOR PREPARATION, PRESENTATION, AND FOLLOW-UP

Preparation
- i–iv–V^7–i

Presentation
- Cut time
- Relative minor scale
- Natural and harmonic minor scales—A minor
- Subdominant (iv) chord in minor
- i–iv–i–V^7–i
- Chromatic scale

Follow-up
- Sixteenth-note combinations
- Tenuto
- Syncopation
- I–IV–V^7–I
- Chord inversions
- Dominant 7th chord
- Harmonic dictation
- Legato pedal

UNIT 6: OVERVIEW

PAGE	ACTIVITY	PRESENTATION	PREPARATION ▲	SPECIAL ACTIVITY
	Repertoire			
81	Lukey's Boat	Cut time		
84	Can't Catch Me!	A minor scale		YBTJ!
86	The Stormy Sea	i–iv–V^7–i		
92	Turkish Bazaar	Chromatic scale; i–iv–V^7–i		
	Solos			
40	Gremlins	Cut time		
42	Magic Act	Chromatic scale		
44	In an Old Garden			
46	Bob-sled Boogie			
	Finger Gyms			
79	Triple Delight		i–iv–V^7–i	Transpose
82	Scaling in A Minor	Relative minor; natural and harmonic minor scales		
88	Bizarre Bazaar	Chromatic scale		
	Musicianship			
83	Chord Progression Challenge	i–iv–i–V^7–i		Transpose
88	Joshua Fit the Battle of Jericho	i–iv–V^7–i; cut time		Transpose
89	Into Inversions			
	Rhythm			
80	Discovering Cut Time	Cut time		
89	Rhythm Map			
	Ear Skills			
79	Interval Safari–Mystery Melody			
90	Hear, Here!—Harmony			
90	Clapbacks			
90	Playbacks			
91	Major–minor Game			
	Creativity			
91	Inversion Toccata			

TEACHER'S NOTES AND TIPS

Musicianship

Minor Scales

Natural and harmonic minor scales are introduced on p. 82. The minor scales are presented as the "relative" scales to the Major scales that they already know. Fingering for A, D, E, and B minor scales are the same as Group 1 Major scales.

The minor i–iv–i–V^7–i chord progression is presented on p. 83. Encourage your students to apply the Major and minor chord progressions they have learned to folk songs, familiar melodies, and improvised tunes.

The Chromatic Scale

The chromatic scale (p. 88) is presented starting on C. We suggest that students also play the chromatic scale starting on other keys. Many students enjoy the challenge of playing the chromatic scale HT in contrary motion, or with their eyes closed.

Rhythm

Cut Time (Alla breve)

With the introduction of cut time on p. 80, stress the importance of feeling the beat in two to a measure. Many students have trouble with this and will continue to count in $\frac{4}{4}$. The composer's intention, however, is to feel the music with two beats to a measure.

Ear Skills

The ear training and solfège skills learned in *Celebrate Piano!™* help develop the students' sight-reading skills. In *Mystery Melody* (p. 79), the student should first sing the melody with solfège or tone numbers to discover the title (*America* [*My Country 'Tis of Thee*] or *God Save the Queen*).

Encourage your students to use Major and minor chord progressions to harmonize folk songs. It is very important for students to look through a piece before playing and use their inner hearing to get a sense of the melody and rhythm.

Tip:

Turkish Bazaar (p. 92) is a student favorite. This exciting piece combines the chromatic scale, sixteenth notes, and a variety of touches, phrasing, and dynamics for a stunning performance. Help your student evoke the exotic sounds of a *Turkish Bazaar* by emphasizing the dynamics and musical elements. Although this is an animated piece, the student should choose a tempo that allows for even playing of the chromatic scale.

Enrichment Repertoire

For additional Level 4, Unit 6 repertoire, play the following pieces from *Celebration Series®, The Piano Odyssey®*, Piano Repertoire 1:

• *Bourrée in D Minor* by Christoph Graupner
• *The Sewing Machine* by Mel. Bonis
• *Hallowe'en Night* by Linda Niamath
• *Beaver Boogie* by Stephen Chatman
• *Robots* by Anne Crosby

Summary

As a graduate of *Celebrate Piano!™*, your student will have a strong musical background, excellent reading and rhythmic skills, and a thorough understanding of ear skills and creativity.

It is our hope that students will continue to use and develop their skills in reading, musicianship, technique, harmonizing, transposition, ear training, and creativity as they pursue a wide variety of musical paths. A thorough grounding in comprehensive musicianship provides the platform for a lifetime of learning and musical enjoyment.